SCIENCE EXPERIMENTS

CHEMISTRY AND PHYSICS

BY
TAMMY K. WILLIAMS

COPYRIGHT © 1995 by Mark Twain Media, Inc.

ISBN # 1-58037-074-8

Printing No. CD–1815

Mark Twain Media, Inc., Publishers
Distributed by Carson-Dellosa Publishing Company, Inc.

CONTENTS

INTRODUCTION

Models, chemical indicators, and carefully monitored experiments are all tools of scientists. In order to understand our world and the elements that make it up, scientists resort to the use of models, experiments done on a smaller scale, carefully controlled conditions, and evidence gathered to support large, complicated theories.

These scientific tools are all evident throughout this activity book as the physics and chemistry of the earth are explored. A unit to review and strengthen laboratory skills is also included.

In the laboratory skills section, objects are classified by different appearances, experiments are conducted to measure a water droplet's splatter size and a ball's bounce height, balloon rockets are constructed, and, finally, an edible test of measurement skills is conducted.

In the chemistry section, hydrogen gas is created from a chemical reaction, collected in a balloon, and exploded. Red cabbage is boiled to make an acid/base indicator, salt is separated from salt water, and soap is made in the classroom.

In the physics unit, the decay of "radioactive" particles is simulated, marbles reflect like light, convex and concave lenses are made from water drops, and a soup can becomes an "eye" and later is turned into a simple motor powered by a battery.

Each of these scientific tools—models, carefully controlled experiments, and simulations—is critical in helping the scientist in each of us to understand the world around us. Enjoy the activities, and don't be afraid to get your hands dirty.

"You learn to do what you do and not something else."

Gerald Unks, Ed 41, UNC-CH, 1984

LABORATORY SKILLS INDEX AND MATERIALS LIST

Date: _____ Names: _____

CLASSIFICATION

INTRODUCTION: How do scientists decide that crocodiles belong in one family of organisms while alligators belong in another family?

OBJECTIVE: In science, organisms are grouped according to different or similar characteristics. This process, called classification, allows for the study of the similarities and differences between organisms. In this activity, we will practice classifying a set of colored and marked cards in order to examine the flexibility that exists when classifying things.

PROCEDURE:
1. A set of marked colored cards are in the envelope provided.
2. Your goal is to design as many classification systems for those cards as possible.
3. As you decide on a classification system:
   a. Arrange the cards into the system.
   b. In the chart below, identify CATEGORIES and MEMBERS in the spaces provided. Members may be drawn in or described.
   c. Draw vertical lines in the charts to separate categories.
   d. List all the members of a category in the column below the category name.

Example: SYSTEM 1: _Classify by shape_____   SYSTEM 2: _____

CATEGORIES	square	circle	rectangle
M E M B E R S	A2 / B1	B2 / A1	(blank) / B1

Date: _____ Names: _____

SYSTEM 3: _____

CATEGORIES [ ]

M
E
M
B
E
R
S

SYSTEM 4: _____

[ ]

SYSTEM 5: _____

CATEGORIES [ ]

M
E
M
B
E
R
S

SYSTEM 6: _____

[ ]

Date: _____ Names: _____

SYSTEM 7:_____ SYSTEM 8: _____

CATEGORIES

M

E

M

B

E

R

S

QUESTIONS:

1. What characteristics about the cards did you use in order to classify them?

_____

_____

2. Does each classification system contain the same categories? Why/why not?

_____

_____

3. Do all categories contain the same members? Why/why not?_____

_____

_____

4. Do you think that each group in the class thought of the same classification systems that you did? _____

_____

5. Do you think that each group in the class would agree on the same system as THE BEST SYSTEM? Why/why not? _____

_____

_____

6. Why then is it important for scientists to agree on a single classification system for each particular group of items/organisms? _____

_____

_____

Date: _____   Names: _____

METRIC MEASUREMENT (LENGTH)

INTRODUCTION: If your hand is 3 inches wide, how many centimeters wide is it? Which metric unit is closest to the length of 1 yard?

OBJECTIVE: In this activity, we will review metric units for measuring distance or length—the meter, decimeter, centimeter, and millimeter. We will also use these units to estimate and then measure the sizes of various objects around the room.

Meterstick: 1 meter (m) = 10 decimeters (dm) OR 100 centimeters (cm) OR 1,000 millimeters (mm)
Here is a visual representation of a meterstick.

| 0   10   20   30   40   50   60   70   80   90   100 cm |

0–1 is 1 centimeter   1 decimeter   ** 1 millimeter is the distance between each tiny black mark on a meterstick.

PROCEDURE: 1. Use a meterstick to measure the objects listed in the chart below. Make sure you use the metric side of the meterstick (with numbers to 100 cm, not 36 inches).
                 2. Measure the objects in the units listed. Write the unit abbreviation after the measurement you get (example: instead of 47.5, write 47.5 cm).

OBJECT	MEASUREMENT	UNITS
Length of your table		Meters (m)
Width of your table		Decimeters (dm)
Length of a piece of paper		Centimeters (cm)
Width/thickness of a pencil		Millimeters (mm)

3. Which unit above is closest to the following size:
   a. the thickness of a fingernail? _____
   b. the width of a finger? _____
   c. the width of a hand? _____
   d. longer than your leg? _____

Date: _____ Names: _____

4. Keep the sizes of each of the metric units in mind. For each object listed in the chart below:

    a. Choose the most appropriate unit of measurement (m, dm, cm, mm) and record that unit in the chart in the "Unit Chosen" column.

    b. Estimate the size of that object using the units you choose and the "body parts" in steps 3a–d above. You may actually lay fingers side-by-side along an object to see how many centimeters long it is. Record your estimates in the chart below under the "Estimate" column.

    c. Get up and measure the objects listed using the units that you chose. Record your measurements in the chart below the "Measurement" column. You do not have to measure the items in the order listed.

OBJECT	UNIT CHOSEN	ESTIMATE (WITH UNITS)	MEASUREMENT (WITH UNITS)
Height of table			
Length of tabletop			
Height of classroom door			
Thickness of tabletop			
Width of cabinets			
Thickness of a pencil lead			
Width of your table leg			

QUESTIONS:

1. Which unit might be best used to measure: a. shoe length? _____

    b. thickness of hair strands? _____

    c. a bus length? _____

    d. width of a door? _____

    e. length of a hallway? _____

    f. height of the letter "E"? _____

    g. length of a pencil?_____

2. How is the metric system simpler to use than English units (like inches, feet, and yards)?

_____

Date: _____   Names: _____

METRIC MEASUREMENT (VOLUME)

INTRODUCTION: The volume of a cube can be calculated by multiplying its length times its width
times its height. How could you figure out the volume of a rock that has broken and
chipped edges? How could you figure out the volume of a bag of marbles without
doing a lot of math?

OBJECTIVE: In this activity, we will learn how to read the volume of a liquid in a graduated cylinder
measuring milliliters (mL) by reading the meniscus of the liquid (see diagram below).
When most liquids are placed in tall, narrow containers, they tend to creep up the
walls of the container a little due to capillary action. This results in the surface of the
liquid appearing to be curved. The bottom of this curve is known as the MENISCUS,
and it best represents the actual volume of liquid in the cylinder. We will also learn
how to measure the volume of odd-shaped objects.

Graduated cylinder:

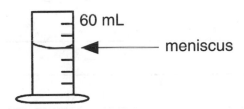

60 mL

◄—— meniscus

PROCEDURE: 1. Pour the colored liquid from the beaker at your lab station into the graduated
cylinder.

2. Sit the graduated cylinder flat on the countertop.

3. Bend over so that the water level is at eye level and look for the meniscus.

4. Record the number of milliliters of liquid (to the nearest one-half mL) in the
chart on the next page. This step will be done before each object is lowered
into the liquid. Since this prepares us to measure the first object, record the
liquid volume in the first box under "Beginning Volume" (second column).

5. Once a starting liquid volume has been measured, gently lower an object
into the liquid. The amount that the water rises (amount of water displaced)
is equal to the volume of the object.

6. Read the new volume at the meniscus and record it in the chart under
"Volume of Liquid & Object" for that object (first column).

7. To calculate the volume of the object alone, subtract the "Beginning
Volume" from the "Volume of Liquid & Object" (column 2 from column 1).

8. Repeat the above steps for each of the remaining objects.

Date: _____ Names: _____

OBJECT	VOLUME OF LIQUID & OBJECT	–	BEGINNING VOLUME (LIQUID)	=	VOLUME OF OBJECT
Nail					
Screw					
Penny					
Rock					

QUESTIONS:

1. Why is it necessary to recheck the starting volume of liquid before each object is put in?

_____

_____

_____

2. What kind of error would result if you read the liquid volume where the liquid touches the wall of the cylinder rather than at the meniscus?

_____

_____

_____

3. How does this "measuring volume by difference" method compare with measuring volume using math for these odd-shaped objects?

_____

_____

_____

_____

Date: _____   Names: _____

METRIC MEASUREMENT (MASS/WEIGHT)

INTRODUCTION: How can you figure out how much of your pencil gets "eaten" by a pencil sharpener each time you sharpen a pencil? How can you figure out how large a gulp of water is?

OBJECTIVE: In this activity, we will become familiar with the parts of a triple-beam balance that is used to measure mass, and we will practice measuring the mass of different objects. Following this, we will learn how to "weigh-by-difference" to find the mass of different objects.

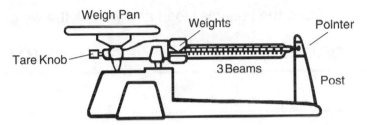

PROCEDURE:

To "ZERO A BALANCE"

1. Check to make sure that the balance is clean. Wipe and clean it if necessary.

2. Move all weights to the left of the balance (next to the weigh pan).

3. Look to see if the pointer line is perfectly in line with the mark on the post. This indicates whether the balance is zeroed.

4. If the lines do not meet, adjust the tare knob, which is located underneath the weigh pan, by turning it a little and observing its effect. You should be able to zero the balance by repeating this procedure.
** If you cannot zero the balance, ASK FOR ASSISTANCE!

To Weigh Objects

1. Use the following steps to weigh each object listed in the chart (in grams), and record its weight in the chart.

2. Make sure the balance is zeroed and the weigh pan is clean.

3. Place an object on the weigh pan.

4. Move the weights on the beams until the pointer just balances at the white mark on the post. Do this by first moving the small weight to the right. If it is too light to balance the object, move it back to the left (to 0) and try the next larger weight. Continue this until one of the weights can be placed so that the pointer is both above and below the post line.
** Make sure that the two larger weights fall into notches as you move them on the beams.

Date: _____ Names: _____

5. Weights can be measured as accurately as the nearest tenth of a gram by positioning the smallest weight.

6. Once the weights have been positioned so that the beam pointer aligns with the mark on the post, add each of the marked weights together to get a total. Remember, the smallest weight marks single grams, and the lines between the numbers on that beam mark tenths of grams. The medium-sized weight marks tens of grams, and the largest weight marks hundreds of grams.

7. Record the total mass in the chart below under "Weight." Write in units.

8. Store the balance clean and with all the weights on zero.

OBJECT	WEIGHT (IN GRAMS)
Small paper clip	
2 small paper clips	
Large paper clip	
2 large paper clips	
One penny	
Empty beaker	
Something you choose: _____	

To Weigh By Difference
1. When doing this, we will be weighing an object, taking away some of or adding to the object, and then reweighing the object to see how much was taken away or added.

2. First, weigh each of the objects listed in the chart on page 11. Record their weights under the column "Weight Before."

3. For each object remove or add to it by: a. putting the sponge in water.
   b. drinking a swallow of water from the cup.
   c. sharpening the pencil.

4. Reweigh each item after step 3 and record its new weight under "Weight After."

Date: _____   Names: _____

5. To find the amount of change (weight gained or lost), subtract the smaller number from the larger number. If the starting number is larger, the weight was lost. If the ending weight was larger, then the weight was gained.

6. Include the units as well as whether weight was gained or lost.

7. Store the balance clean and dry and with all weights on zero.

OBJECT	WEIGHT BEFORE	WEIGHT AFTER	WEIGHT CHANGE (GRAMS)
Dry sponge (put in water)			
Cup of water (take a sip)			
Pencil (sharpened)			

QUESTIONS:

1. Why is it important to make sure that the weigh pan is clean before weighing objects?

_____

_____

_____

2. How does "weighing by difference" compare to something like saving pencil shavings and weighing them to find out how much is sharpened off? _____

_____

_____

_____

_____

_____

Date: _____ Names: _____

MAKING A HYPOTHESIS

INTRODUCTION: Do you know what will happen if you mix vinegar and baking soda? Will the temperature change? Will bubbles form? Guessing what will happen is called making a hypothesis.

OBJECTIVE: A hypothesis is a "best guess" because the outcome of a question is guessed using only what is known before the question is tested. The hypothesis is then tested using experiments. During the experiment, data or information is collected to check the accuracy of the hypothesis. Finally, using the results of the experiment, the hypothesis may be supported as correct or it may be changed. In this activity, we will make hypotheses about how combining liquids with two different chemicals will affect the temperature of each liquid.

PROCEDURE: <u>CHEMICAL A AND WATER</u>

1. Place your hypothesis for "Chemical A and Water" below. What do you think will happen?

2. Measure 5 mL of water in the graduated cylinder and pour it into a test tube.
3. Place the test tube in the test tube rack and gently place the thermometer in the water in the test tube.
4. After 1 minute, record the temperature of the water and record this temperature in the chart on page 13 under "Start."
5. Using the metal spatula, add 3 pellets of "Chemical A" to your test tube. DO NOT TOUCH THE PELLETS WITH YOUR SKIN!
6. Observe and record the temperature of the water every 15 seconds for 3 minutes.
7. At the end of 3 minutes, remove the thermometer, pour the contents of the test tube down the drain, and rinse the test tube and thermometer.
8. Graph the data from the chart on the graph sheet on the next page. Use a SOLID LINE to connect the dots of data.

<u>CHEMICAL B AND VINEGAR</u>

9. Place your hypothesis for "Chemical B and Vinegar" below. What do you think will happen?

10. Repeat the exact procedure used for Chemical A, EXCEPT:
    a. In #2 above, begin with 5 mL of vinegar.
    b. In #5 above, add 1/2 teaspoon of "Chemical B."
11. Graph the data for Chemical B on the graph on the next page. Use a BROKEN LINE to connect the data points.

Date: _____ Names: _____

DATA:

TEMPERATURE CHANGE (DEGREES CELSIUS)

Time (seconds)

	Start	15	30	45	60	75	90	105	120	135	150	165	180
CHEMICAL A													
CHEMICAL B													

TEMPERATURE VERSUS TIME

TIME (SECONDS)

Date: _____ Names: _____

QUESTIONS:

1. What happened to the water temperature when Chemical A was added?

_____

2. What happened to the vinegar temperature when Chemical B was added?

_____

3. How did your hypothesis for Chemical A compare to your results?

_____

_____

_____

4. How did your hypothesis for Chemical B compare to your results?

_____

_____

_____

5. What do scientists need to do before accepting their hypotheses?

_____

_____

6. Why was a starting temperature needed?

_____

_____

_____

7. What are the two most noticeable observations about what happens when baking soda (Chemical B) and vinegar are mixed?

_____

_____

_____

_____

Date: _____   Names: _____

SCIENTIFIC METHOD:
SHAPE OF WATER SPLATTER VERSUS DROP HEIGHT

INTRODUCTION: If you dribble Kool-Aid while you are standing when you pour it, will it splatter more or less than if you are sitting when you pour it?

OBJECTIVE: In this activity, we will practice using the scientific method while investigating the effect of drop height on the size and shape of water droplet splatters when they land. We will be careful to change only the one item whose effect we will observe. This is called the EXPERIMENTAL VARIABLE. All of the other conditions must be kept completely identical. These conditions are called CONTROLS.

PROCEDURE: 1. As you follow the instructions to complete the investigation below, fill in the steps of the scientific method by writing in what you do at each step in the water droplet investigation where it matches a step in the scientific method.

STATE PROBLEM: _____

_____

GATHER INFORMATION (name sources of information):

a. _____   b. _____

c. _____   d. _____

MAKE HYPOTHESIS: _____

_____

EXPERIMENT: _____

_____

_____

RECORD DATA (list examples of data): a. _____

b. _____   c. _____

FORM CONCLUSION: _____

_____

Date: _____   Names: _____

2. Add 2 drops of food coloring to your beaker.

3. Add 100 mL of water and mix.

4. Partially fill the glass dropper with colored water.

5. Measure the heights listed in the chart using a meterstick positioned with one end on the splatter paper and the other end measuring dropper height.

6. From each height, drop 3 drops of water (in different places on the paper).

7. Measure the size of the splatter in MILLIMETERS, and record each trial size in the chart. Add the sizes to get a total, and divide by 3 to find the average size of each splatter.

8. Repeat this process for each height.

9. For each drop height, write a description of the splatter in the chart, also. Examples: "Drop is very round," "Drop broke apart," or "Drop is surrounded by little splatters."

10. On the graph, plot the average splatter size versus drop height.

DATA:

DIAMETER OF DROP SPLATTERS (mm)

Drop Height	Trial 1	Trial 2	Trial 3	Total	Average	Description
5 cm						
10 cm						
20 cm						
40 cm						
80 cm						

Date: _____   Names: _____

DROP HEIGHT VERSUS SPLATTER SIZE

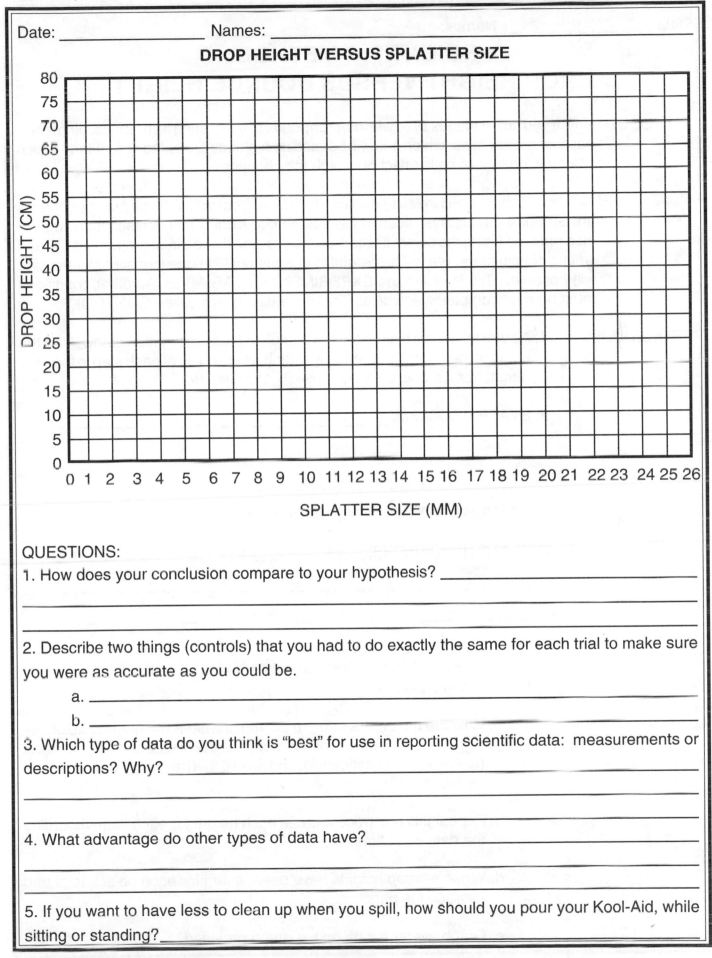

QUESTIONS:

1. How does your conclusion compare to your hypothesis? _____

_____

_____

2. Describe two things (controls) that you had to do exactly the same for each trial to make sure

you were as accurate as you could be.

     a. _____

     b. _____

3. Which type of data do you think is "best" for use in reporting scientific data: measurements or

descriptions? Why? _____

_____

_____

4. What advantage do other types of data have?_____

_____

_____

5. If you want to have less to clean up when you spill, how should you pour your Kool-Aid, while

sitting or standing?_____

Date: _____   Names: _____

SCIENTIFIC METHOD:
DROP HEIGHT VERSUS BOUNCE HEIGHT

INTRODUCTION: If you spill a toybox filled with different kinds of balls, such as marbles, ping-pong balls, or rubber balls, which one will bounce up highest? Does the height from which you spill the box of balls affect how high they bounce?

OBJECTIVE: In this activity, we will investigate how the height from which three types of objects are dropped affects their bounce heights. In conducting this investigation, we will also practice using the scientific method: conducting three trials, graphing data, and writing conclusions. We will be careful to change only the one item whose effect we will observe. This is called the EXPERIMENTAL VARIABLE. All other conditions must be kept completely identical. These conditions are called CONTROLS.

PROCEDURE:

1. As you follow the instructions to complete the investigation below, fill in the steps of the scientific method by writing what you do at each step in the drop height versus bounce height investigation.

2. STATE PROBLEM: _____

_____

_____

GATHER INFORMATION (skip this item)

3. STATE HYPOTHESIS: _____

_____

_____

4. EXPERIMENT (see below):

   a. From each of the identified heights listed in the chart, drop each of the three items.

   b. Hold the meterstick straight up and measure the bounce height by sight. Measure the maximum height of the first bounce of the object (to the nearest centimeter), and record this height in the appropriate data chart.

   c. Repeat this test twice more at each height for each item, recording the data each time.

   d. When all drop heights have been tested for each object, total and average the data.

   e. Graph average data on the graph provided.

18

Date: _____ Names: _____

5. RECORD DATA:

Item 1: _____

Drop Height   Bounce Height

Drop Height	Trial 1	Trial 2	Trial 3	Total	Average
10 cm					
20 cm					
30 cm					
40 cm					
50 cm					
60 cm					
70 cm					
80 cm					
90 cm					
100 cm					

Item 2: _____

Drop Height   Bounce Height

Drop Height	Trial 1	Trial 2	Trial 3	Total	Average
10 cm					
20 cm					
30 cm					
40 cm					
50 cm					
60 cm					
70 cm					
80 cm					
90 cm					
100 cm					

Item 3: _____

Drop Height   Bounce Height

Drop Height	Trial 1	Trial 2	Trial 3	Total	Average
10 cm					
20 cm					
30 cm					
40 cm					
50 cm					
60 cm					
70 cm					
80 cm					
90 cm					
100 cm					

Date: _____ Names: _____

6. FORM CONCLUSION: _____

_____

7. CREATE A LINE GRAPH showing the average data for each of the three objects.

AVERAGE DROP HEIGHT VERSUS BOUNCE HEIGHT

DROP HEIGHT (CM)

BOUNCE HEIGHT (CM)

QUESTIONS:

1. What is the experimental variable for this experiment? _____

2. What are three controls for this experiment? a._____

                                                     b._____

                                                     c._____

3. Which of the balls that you tested was most likely to:

    a. bounce low and stay near where it was dropped? _____

    b. bounce high and bounce away from where it was dropped? _____

Date: _____ Names: _____

SCIENTIFIC METHOD:
ROCKET ENGINES AND NEWTON'S THIRD LAW

INTRODUCTION: What would happen if you stood still while wearing skates and threw baseballs away from you? Would you move? How about if you sat on a skateboard and did the same thing?

OBJECTIVE: Newton's Third Law says that for every action there is an equal and opposite reaction. This means that if you push someone away from you, you are pushed backwards with the same force that you exerted. In the same manner, if a rocket's exhaust exerts 150 newtons of force against a concrete launch pad, the same force is exerted on the rocket. This is what causes the rocket to be lifted into the air. In this activity, we will investigate this reaction using a balloon as the engine and a straw as the rocket. We will be careful to change only the one item whose effect we will observe. This is called the experimental variable. All other conditions must be kept completely identical. These conditions are called controls.

PROCEDURE:
    A. STATE PROBLEM: _____

_____

    B. GATHER INFORMATION (skip this section)

    C. FORM HYPOTHESIS: _____

_____

    D. EXPERIMENT (see procedure below):
        1. Attach your flight string to the wall opposite you across the room, and pull your string level. String should be 4–6 meters long.
        2. Inflate your balloon to the 3-cm diameter indicated in the chart.
        3. Hold the balloon closed or close it in some other way SO THAT IT CAN BE QUICKLY REOPENED LATER.

Tape   Mark on string   Open end toward you

        4. Attach the balloon to the straw, OPEN END TOWARD YOU, CLOSED END TOWARD THE BOARD. (See diagram.)
        5. Facing the string attachment, hold the flight string level near its end.
        6. Start the straw at the mark on the string.
        7. Release the rocket (balloon) and allow it to fly down the string.
        8. Holding the string level, measure the distance traveled by the rocket.
        9. Repeat steps 1–8 twice more for this diameter and record the data in the chart.
        10. Repeat entire procedure for each diameter in the chart.
        11. Graph average distances versus balloon diameter on a computer. Attach your graph printout sheets to your lab sheet. If you don't have access to a computer, use the graph provided on page 22.

Date: _____   Names: _____

E. RECORD DATA:

Diameter of Balloon   **Distance Traveled by Balloon**

	Trial 1	Trial 2	Trial 3	Total	Average
3 cm					
6 cm					
9 cm					
12 cm					
15 cm					

F. FORM CONCLUSION: _____

_____

_____

QUESTIONS:

1. What is the experimental variable in this experiment? _____

2. Name three controls for this experiment: a. _____

b. _____   c. _____

3. How would Newton's Third Law affect you if you threw baseballs away from you while standing on skates or sitting on a skateboard? _____

_____

_____

BALLOON DIAMETER VERSUS FLIGHT DISTANCE

FLIGHT DISTANCE (M)

7.5 –
7.0 –
6.5 –
6.0 –
5.5 –
5.0 –
4.5 –
4.0 –
3.5 –
3.0 –
2.5 –
2.0 –
1.5 –
1.0 –
.5 –
0 –

0   3   6   9   12   15

BALLOON DIAMETER (CM)

Date: _____   Names: _____

LAB TECHNIQUES GOOD ENOUGH TO EAT

INTRODUCTION: How is cooking similar to chemistry? Both involve following directions well enough to avoid catastrophe!

OBJECTIVE: In this activity, we will practice measuring length, mass, and volume using metric units. The end product will be an indicator of your ability to measure accurately. If your measurement skills are very good, your result will be good enough to eat!

PROCEDURE:

1. Measure 16 cm from the bottom of the large plastic bag and use the pen at your lab station to mark the height.

2. Fill the bag to the line that you marked with ice (from the cooler).

3. MEASURE out 100 mL of ROCK SALT, and pour it over the ice in the large bag.

4. Take a new, small plastic bag and mix the following ingredients into this bag:
   a. 100 mL MILK
   b. 20 mL SUGAR
   c. 2 drops of VANILLA EXTRACT

5. Seal the contents of the small bag (make sure the bag is "ziplocked").

6. Place the small bag inside the large bag of ice.

7. Seal the large bag (with the small bag inside). Make sure the bag is "ziplocked."

8. Move the ice in the large bag around so that it surrounds/covers/supports the small bag.

9. Time 1-minute intervals. At the end of each 1-minute interval, turn the bag over onto the other side. (Arrange ice cubes so that they surround the small bag inside.)

10. Repeat the 1-minute "flippings" a total of 10 times.

11. At the end of the 10th minute (10 1-minute flips), time 30-second intervals and flip the bag every 30 seconds for 5 minutes (10 30-second flips).

12. At the end of the 20 flips (10 flips 1 minute apart and 10 flips 30 seconds apart), ask your instructor to check to see if your solution has completed its reaction.

Date: _____ Names: _____

13. A. If your solution is approved, you may eat your solution . . . IF YOU DARE!

B. If your solution is not approved, continue flipping every 30 seconds for an additional 5 minutes. Then you may complete step 13A.

**THIS MAY ALSO BE DONE WITH A BABY FOOD JAR INSIDE A COFFEE CAN WITH A PLASTIC RECLOSEABLE LID. IN THIS SET-UP, ALTERNATE HANDFULS OF ICE AND SALT AND THEN ROLL CAN UNDER FOOT.

Flip Checklist (X out numbers as you flip)

1-MINUTE FLIPS	1	2	3	4	5	6	7	8	9	10
30-SECOND FLIPS	1	2	3	4	5	6	7	8	9	10

QUESTIONS:

1. What solution do you end up with? _____

2. Instead of an explosion, what might result if you measure inaccurately?

_____

_____

_____

3. Besides successful science experiments, list two other areas where good measurement skills are important.

a. _____

b. _____

LABORATORY SKILLS ANSWER KEYS

CLASSIFICATION (page 4)

1. Answers will vary, but will include color, size, print color, letters or numbers on them, and so on.
2. No. The system determines what categories will be necessary.
3. No. Category members are determined by the system used.
4. Not exactly, but there will be a lot of overlap because some systems are easy to figure out.
5. No. Different people will prefer different characteristics.
6. Scientists should agree on a best system because it lessens confusion when trying to organize data.

METRIC MEASUREMENT (LENGTH) (pages 5–6)

3a. millimeter
  b. centimeter
  c. decimeter
  d. meter
1. Some range of error should be allowed for answers given.
  a. dm/cm
  b. mm
  c. m
  d. dm
  e. m
  f. mm
  g. cm/dm
2. The metric system is based on units of 10 so you can change from one unit to another simply by dividing or multiplying by 10. In the English system, you have to use 3, 12, 36, and so on.

METRIC MEASUREMENT (VOLUME) (page 8)

1. Water is removed with the object in each trial so the starting volume decreases and may result in a larger end volume being recorded if a new starting volume is not recorded.
2. The volume would be read higher than it actually is.
3. "Measuring by difference" is a lot easier than trying to calculate the volume using math.

METRIC MEASUREMENT (MASS/WEIGHT) (page 11)

1. A dirty weigh pan means you are weighing dirt and the starting weight is read higher than it should be.
2. "Weighing by difference" is easier than saving shavings (that blow away and stick to stuff).

MAKING A HYPOTHESIS (page 14)
1. The temperature increased.
2. The temperature decreased.
3. Will be determined by hypothesis. Hypothesis will be supported or will not be supported by data.
4. Same as #3.
5. Scientists must test their hypotheses.
6. Without a starting temperature, you won't know if the temperature increases or decreases.
7. Answers may vary, but will probably include: "The solution bubbles over, and the temperature drops."

SCIENTIFIC METHOD: SHAPE OF WATER SPLATTER VERSUS DROP HEIGHT (page 17)
1. Will be determined by hypothesis. Data will either support or not support the hypothesis.
2a. meterstick had to be held exactly straight up;
  b. you had to measure from same point on dropper each time; other controls are acceptable.
3. Measurements are probably best because they can be replicated exactly by different scientists.
4. Other data, like descriptions, give information that measurements do not (like shape).
5. Pour Kool-Aid while sitting.

SCIENTIFIC METHOD: DROP HEIGHT VERSUS BOUNCE HEIGHT (page 20)
1. Drop height
2a. meterstick was held perfectly upright;
  b. measurement was made from bottom of each ball;
  c. drop was made onto same surface each time
3a. lowest bouncing ball (determined by items used and data recorded)
  b. highest bouncing ball (determined by items used and data recorded)

SCIENTIFIC METHOD: ROCKET ENGINES AND NEWTON'S THIRD LAW (page 22)
1. Balloon diameter
2a. measuring from same end of straw each time;
  b. holding string perfectly level each time;
  c. not allowing rocket to move until measurement is complete each time
3. When you have no friction holding you in place, throwing objects one direction will push you in the opposite direction.

LAB TECHNIQUES GOOD ENOUGH TO EAT (page 24)
1. Ice cream
2. Bad-tasting ice cream would result.
3a. following a recipe when cooking;
  b. cutting out pieces of a pattern/puzzle; other items may be accepted.

CHEMISTRY INDEX AND MATERIALS LIST

Safety goggles, water, aluminum foil, sodium hydroxide (NaOH), metal spatula, plastic spoon, Erlenmeyer flask, balloons, triple-beam balance, weigh boats, string, marking pen, wood splint, and meterstick.

Chromatography paper (or coffee filter), 2 test tubes, acetone, black marker, and green marker.

Ice, chemical thermometer, beaker, Bunsen burner, ring stand, safety goggles, and timer.

Litmus paper and color chart, red cabbage, 2 beakers, water, beaker tongs, Bunsen burner, ring stand, safety goggles, droppers, solutions listed in chart on page 37, phenolphthalein, weak acid, and weak base.

Ice cubes, Bunsen burner, ring stand, water, salt, chemical thermometer, beakers, metal spatula, triple-beam balance, and weigh boats.

1.0 M silver nitrate solution, copper wire (uninsulated), and small disposable plastic or paper dish or cup.

1. 1.0 M silver nitrate ($AgNO_3$) solution: Add 17 grams of $AgNO_3$ to enough water to make 100 mL total and stir to dissolve.
2. If too much silver precipitates or you want to cut costs, cut the amout of silver nitrate added to the water in half (0.5 M).
3. Leftover solution can be collected and reused. More silver nitrate may be added to increase the concentration, as a precise concentration is not needed.

Iron chloride, sodium hydroxide (NaOH), graduated cylinder, and 250-mL beaker.

1. 1% iron chloride solution: Add 1.7 grams of $FeCl_3 \cdot 6H_2O$ to 100 mL of water (distilled or deionized if possible). [It is 1.7 g $FeCl_3$/100 mL of water due to the H_2O in the formula.] If there is solid on the bottom when you go to use it, it is okay to use the solution on top (clear yellow), or shake the solution, which gives a cloudy suspension.
2. 0.10 M sodium hydroxide solution: Add 4.0 grams of NaOH to 100 mL of water.
3. Adjust amounts above accordingly if you want more or less solution. A 100 mL beaker or larger is fine.
4. These directions give a nice fluffy, orange precipitate. Upon standing, the solid settles and the solution above is nearly colorless.
5. You could also try 5 mL of 0.1 M iron chloride solution (Add 2.7 grams of $FeCl_3 \cdot 6H_2O$ to 100 mL of water.) plus 10 mL of 0.50 M sodium bydroxide solution (Add 20.0 grams of NaOH to 100 mL of water.) and then stir or swirl. This gives a fine, red precipitate.

Date: _____ Names:_____

MAKING HYDROGEN GAS

INTRODUCTION: What happens when you shake up a soft drink? What are the bubbles made of? Will other reactions produce gases (other than carbon dioxide), as well?

OBJECTIVE: In this activity, we will produce hydrogen gas from a chemical reaction and then observe a very distinguishable characteristic of this gas.

PROCEDURE:

1. **Safety goggles must be worn at all times during this experiment!**
2. Measure 50 mL water and pour it into the flask at your lab station.
3. Weigh 0.6 g of aluminum foil, tear the foil into pieces, wad the pieces into small, loosely formed balls, and drop them into the flask of water.
4. Take your weigh boat to the supply station and, using your metal spatula and plastic spoon, count out 10 pellets of sodium hydroxide (NaOH). Add this to the flask.
5. Gently swirl the solution in the flask so that the aluminum is wet.
6. Stretch the mouth of a balloon over the opening of the flask.
7. Observe and record observations for 10 minutes.
8. At the end of 10 minutes, remove the balloon from the flask without letting the gas out of the balloon and tie the balloon closed. Your instructor will help you if needed.
9. Write your names on your balloon with a felt tipped pen, and turn it in to your instructor.
10. Clean up your lab station and have a seat for your instructor's final demonstration with your balloon. (The instructor will touch the balloon with a burning wood splint attached to the end of a meterstick—in a large cleared space.)
11. Sketch the set-up as it appears before and after the reaction in the space below.

BEFORE:

AFTER:

OBSERVATIONS: A. _____

B. _____

C. _____

D. _____

Date: _____ Names: _____

QUESTIONS:

1. What happened to the balloon on top of the flask? _____

_____

2. (H_2O + NaOH + Al) is the formula of chemicals added together in this experiment. Where might the hydrogen gas have come from?

_____

_____

3. What major identifying characteristic did you observe about hydrogen gas? _____

_____

4. Why do you think hydrogen is no longer used for hot air balloons and blimps (helium is used instead)?

_____

_____

5. Do you think the carbon dioxide from your soft drink bottle would react the same as hydrogen when exposed to a flame? Why?

_____

_____

Date: _____   Names: _____

WHAT COLOR IS BLACK?
DO YELLOW AND BLUE MAKE GREEN?

INTRODUCTION: Is green ink only green? Can you separate it to see if yellow and blue make it green? What color is black ink really?

OBJECTIVE: In this activity, you will separate black and green inks to see what colors they are made of. You will use a process called CHROMATOGRAPHY. Chromatography is a process of separating a substance into its parts (which are usually colored). This will be done on a piece of filter paper. (Coffee filters can be used instead of filter paper.)

PROCEDURE:

1. Trim the filter paper provided so that it has the dimensions of the paper in the diagram at right. It should be long enough to stick out of the test tube (approx. 20 cm).
2. Cut a small notch on either side of the bottom end of the filter paper as shown at right.
3. On one sheet of filter paper, place a dot just above the notch in the middle of the paper using a **black** marker. (Make several more dots on top of the first dot to make sure there is a lot of ink there.)
4. Blow the dot dry for about 1 minute.
5. Repeat steps 1–4 for the **green** ink on the other filter paper.
6. Pour 5 mL of **acetone** into each of your 2 test tubes.
7. Hang 1 piece of filter paper inside each test tube so that only the end of the filter paper below the notch is in the acetone.
8. Place the test tubes in the test tube rack for about 15 minutes and observe the reaction. Record observations every 3 minutes in the chart below.

INK	3 MINUTES	6 MINUTES	9 MINUTES	12 MINUTES	15 MINUTES
Black					
Green					

9. At the end of the 15 minutes, remove the pieces of filter paper from test tubes of acetone.
10. Tape each piece of filter paper onto the back of this sheet, and label each of the following:
    a. which ink was applied at the start.
    b. what individual colors can be identified.

Date: _____ Names: _____

QUESTIONS:

1. From your observations, what job do you think the acetone did during this reaction? _____

_____

_____

2. What colors appeared from the separation of the black ink? _____

_____

_____

3. What colors appeared from the separation of the green ink? _____

_____

_____

4. What evidence did you find for the following statement: "Green objects appear green because they absorb all colors of light except green"?

_____

_____

5. What do you think causes some colored pigments to travel higher up the filter paper?

_____

_____

_____

6. Why did you have to be careful not to let your ink dot touch the acetone? What would have been the result if you had?

_____

_____

_____

_____

Date: _____ Names: _____

TEMPERATURE AND CHANGE OF STATE

INTRODUCTION: If you hold an ice cube in your hand, it will begin to melt, but what happens to your hand? Your hand will lose heat to the ice cube.

OBJECTIVE: As the temperature increases within a substance, the molecules within the substance accelerate, and the physical state of the substance will eventually change. For example, as the temperature within an ice cube increases, the atoms within the water molecules begin to move more rapidly, and eventually, the molecules break free of their crystals, push apart, and become liquid. In this activity, we will examine how much increase in temperature is necessary in order for ice to change into water and then for water to change into steam.

PROCEDURE:

1. Place 4–6 ice cubes in a small beaker.

2. Hold a thermometer directly onto an ice cube for 1 minute to record a beginning temperature for the ice.

3. Record this starting temperature in the chart on the next page.

4. Without removing the thermometer from the beaker, place the beaker on the wire mesh on the ring stand.

5. Put on your goggles, and ask your instructor to light your Bunsen burner.

6. Without removing the thermometer, measure the temperature every 30 seconds as the ice melts, the water heats, and then begins to boil.

7. Record all temperatures in the chart.

8. Graph your temperature data on the graph provided, and **label** on the graph line where **melting** and **evaporating** first occur.

Date: _____   Names: _____

DATA:

TIME	TEMPERATURE
Start	
0.5	
1.0	
1.5	
2.0	
2.5	
3.0	
3.5	
4.0	
4.5	
5.0	
5.5	
6.0	
6.5	

TIME	TEMPERATURE
7.0	
7.5	
8.0	
8.5	
9.0	
9.5	
10.0	
10.5	
11.0	
11.5	
12.0	
12.5	
13.0	
13.5	

TIME	TEMPERATURE
14.0	
14.5	
15.0	
15.5	
16.0	
16.5	
17.0	
17.5	
18.0	
18.5	
19.0	
19.5	
20.0	

TEMPERATURE VERSUS TIME

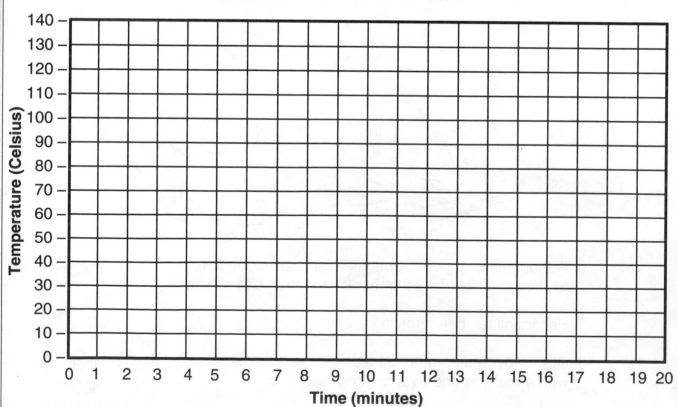

Date: _____ Names: _____

QUESTIONS:

1. According to your data, at what temperature is water in the form of ice?_____

2. According to your data, at what temperature does water boil?_____

3. Look at the graph of your data. What is the temperature range where the ice had just completed

melting? _____

4. Look at the graph of your data. What happens to the temperature as the solution:

   a. completes melting? _____

_____

   b. is boiling continuously? _____

_____

5. What evidence might you have that a "change of state" requires the use of the heat energy that

would otherwise have caused the temperature to increase? _____

_____

6. If the process of melting absorbs heat energy from the surroundings, then what would the

process of freezing do? _____

_____

7. Why do citrus farmers spray water on their crops the evening before the temperature is predicted

to drop below freezing? _____

_____

8. The heat that your hand loses to an ice cube is used to do what? _____

_____

Date: _____ Names: _____

INDICATORS, pH, AND NEUTRALIZATION

INTRODUCTION: Suppose that you found a bottle of clear liquid in the garage at home and you needed to know if it was an acid or a base. Is there any way you can tell?

OBJECTIVE: The pH of a solution is a measure of the balance between two types of ions that are found in the solution. Extra hydronium ions (H_3O+) will cause a solution to be acidic. Extra hydroxide ions (OH-) will cause a solution to be a base. If the ions are equal in the solution, the solution is said to be neutral. pH can be measured very precisely or just enough to determine if a solution is an acid or a base. In this activity, we will test to see if solutions are acid or base by using a liquid indicator we will make from cabbage juice. This indicator is green in a BASE and red in an ACID. Afterwards, we will use litmus paper to test the specific pH of each solution. Using litmus paper, pHs are given as numbers on a scale of 1 to 14. 1–6 are ACIDS, 7 is NEUTRAL, and 8–14 are BASES.

PROCEDURE: <u>INDICATOR TEST</u>

1. Get 5–6 chunks of red cabbage from the container and put them in your 250-mL beaker.

2. Add 150 mL of water to the beaker.

3. Place the beaker on the wire mesh on the ring stand.

4. All group members should put goggles on before asking the instructor to light their Bunsen burner.

5. Once the solution in the beaker begins to boil, allow the boiling to continue for 5 minutes.

6. At the end of 5 minutes, use the tongs to remove the beaker from the ring stand and cut off the gas supply to your Bunsen burner.

7. The liquid in the beaker is now an acid/base indicator.

8. There are 7 solutions available at your lab station. Each should be tested by:
   a. Placing 20 drops (about a pipette full) of one solution into a clean test beaker.

   b. Adding about 10 drops of red cabbage indicator.

   c. Observing the color, identifying whether the solution is acid or base, and recording the data in the chart.

   d. Pouring mixture down the drain, rinsing beaker and pipette, and repeating for the other solutions.

Date: _____ Names: _____

pH TEST

9. To measure the actual pH (level of acidity/basicity) of each solution using litmus paper:

   a. Tear a piece of litmus paper in half.

   b. Dip one end into a solution and remove it immediately.

   c. Compare Its new color with the color chart provided.

   d. Record the pH number that matches the color chart in the chart on the next page, and determine whether the pH number represents acid, base, or neutral.

   e. Discard that litmus paper, and repeat for each new solution.

TEST SOLUTION	COLOR	ACID/BASE/ OR NEUTRAL	pH NUMBER	ACID/BASE/ OR NEUTRAL
Vinegar				
Baking Soda				
Tap Water				
Saliva				
Soft Drink				
Lemon Juice				
Ammonia				

Date: _____ Names: _____

NEUTRALIZATION

10. To neutralize a weak acid solution:

   a. Add 10 drops of acid to a clean beaker.

   b. Add 20 drops of phenolphthalein (an acid/base indicator) to the acid.
   ** Phenolphthalein is clear in an acid and pink in a base. **

   c. Observe the color of the solution. Record your observations below.

   d. Rinse pipette, and add drops of the weak base one at a time, counting as you add them and swirling the solution gently between drops, until the solution changes color and remains (without fading out).

   e. Record the number of drops of base needed to change the color below.

11. The process may be reversed by rinsing the pipette and adding individual drops of acid, counting as you add them and swirling the solution gently between drops, until the color changes back (without fading out). Record this number in the space below.

Original Color of Acid With Phenolphthalein	Number of Drops of Base to Change Color	Color of Base With Phenolphthalein	Number of Drops of Acid to Change Color

Date: _____   Names: _____

QUESTIONS:

1. Was the red cabbage juice (after boiling) acid or base? How do you know?_____

_____

_____

2. Is litmus paper or an indicator better to use to test pH? Why? _____

_____

_____

3. On the pH number scale below, put a **box** around **bases,** an **X** on **neutral,** and a **circle** around the **acids.**

1	2	3	4	5	6	7	8	9	10	11	12	13	14

4. How are acidic solutions different from basic solutions (chemically)? _____

_____

_____

5. What does pH mean?_____

_____

6. Why is it important to know if solutions are acids, bases, or neutrals? _____

_____

_____

_____

Date: _____ Names: _____

TEMPERATURE EFFECTS ON SOLUBILITY

INTRODUCTION: Can you dissolve more sugar in cold tea or in hot tea?

OBJECTIVE: In a solution, there is usually a liquid (SOLVENT) and a solid (SOLUTE) that gets dissolved in the liquid. In this activity, we will experiment to find out how the temperature of a liquid affects how much solid can be dissolved in it. We will also practice weighing by difference to determine the amount of solid dissolved.

OUR HYPOTHESIS:

PROCEDURE:
1. Label the 3 beakers at your lab station COLD, ROOM TEMPERATURE, and HOT.
2. Set up each beaker as follows:
     COLD: Add 100 mL water and as many ice cubes as possible.
     ROOM TEMPERATURE: Add 100 mL tap water.
     HOT: Add 100 mL water and bring to boil on ring stand over Bunsen burner.
3. Weigh out 50 g of salt using the triple-beam balance.
4. Begin with room temperature water and repeat the steps below for the other two temperatures of water, once the cold water reaches its coldest temperature and the hot water has reached boiling. **Do not leave the beaker over the Bunsen burner unattended!**
5. Remove a spatula of salt from the measured 50 g and add to the test temperature beaker.
6. Stir until the salt is completely dissolved.
7. Repeat until you cannot get the salt to dissolve while stirring constantly for about 2 minutes. There will be some grains of salt left on the bottom of the beaker. The solution is now saturated with salt.
8. To find out how much salt was added to the solution:
     a. Place the plastic weigh boat that started out with 50 g of salt (from which you have been getting the salt to add to the water) back on the balance.
     b. Balance the weigh boat on the balance to find its new (lighter) weight.
     c. Record this weight in the chart and subtract this from the original 50 g that you started with.
     d. Record the difference in the chart.
9. Use the thermometer to measure a final temperature of the saturated solution. Record this temperature in the chart.
10. Repeat steps 3–8 for the other two temperatures of water, and record your data in the chart.
11. Graph the salt used at each temperature versus each final temperature on the graph provided.

Date: _____   Names: _____

	ROOM TEMP. WATER	COLD WATER	HOT WATER
Starting Salt	50 g	50 g	50 g
– Ending Salt	–	–	–
Salt Used			
Final Temperature			

TEMPERATURE VERSUS SOLUBILITY

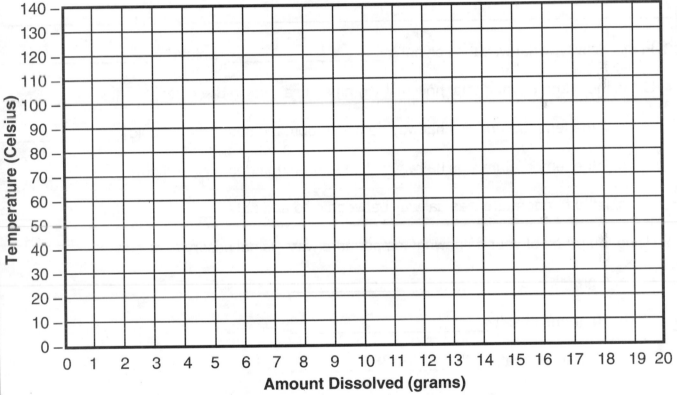

Temperature (Celsius) vs. Amount Dissolved (grams)

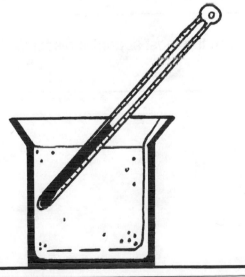

Date: _____ Names: _____

QUESTIONS:

1. How do your results compare to your hypothesis? _____

_____

_____

2. In general, how does the temperature of a liquid affect how much solid will dissolve in it?

_____

_____

3. In this activity, what was the solvent? _____ Solute? _____

4. Using the graph of your data, how many grams of salt would dissolve:

     a. if the temperature was halfway between room temperature and cold? _____

     b. if the temperature was halfway between room temperature and hot? _____

     c. if the temperature was halfway between cold and hot? _____

5. Using the graph of your data, what temperature water is necessary to dissolve:

     a. 5 grams of salt? _____

     b. 10 grams of salt? _____

     c. 15 grams of salt? _____

     d. 20 grams of salt? _____

6. In which temperature tea can the most sugar be dissolved? _____

_____

Date: _____   Names: _____

SINGLE DISPLACEMENT REACTION

INTRODUCTION: What happens to cause metal to become "gold plated" or "silver plated"?

OBJECTIVE: In this activity, we will be adding copper wire to a silver nitrate solution in order to plate silver on the copper wire. The replacement of silver on the copper wire represents a single displacement reaction.

$$AgNO_3 + Cu \longrightarrow CuNO_3 + Ag$$

PROCEDURE:
1. Take a short piece of copper wire and bend it into some unique shape.
2. Place the wire shape into its own small petri dish or paper or plastic cup.
3. Add silver nitrate solution to the petri dish or cup until the wire is just covered.
4. Observe the resulting reaction and record in the space below what you see happening.
5. When the reaction is complete (no more silver is plating) remove the silverplated copper wire from the petri dish or cup using the forceps.
6. Pour the extra silver nitrate solution back into the supply beaker.

** The plated silver is not firmly attached to the copper wire and will rinse off easily. It also is not polished, so it appears grayish-black in color. You may keep it if you like (with the petri dish or cup).

OBSERVATIONS: _____

_____

_____

_____

QUESTIONS:

1. Write out the reaction in words. _____

_____

_____

2. What type of reaction is this? _____

_____

3. Describe how you know what type of reaction this is. _____

_____

_____

Date: _____ Names: _____

DOUBLE DISPLACEMENT REACTION

OBJECTIVE: In this activity, we will observe the reaction that occurs when elements from two different compounds trade places to produce a double displacement reaction.

PROCEDURE:

1. Measure 5 mL of 1% iron chloride solution in the graduated cylinder, and describe its appearance in the chart below.
2. Pour the 5 mL of 1% iron chloride solution into a 250-mL beaker.
3. Rinse the graduated cylinder, measure 10 mL of 0.10 M sodium hydroxide solution, and describe its appearance in the chart below.
4. Gently pour the sodium hydroxide solution into the beaker with the iron chloride solution and gently swirl (or stir with a glass rod).
5. Allow the solution to sit undisturbed for 5 to 10 minutes.
6. Describe the appearance of the final solution in the chart below at the end of the 10 minutes.

$$FeCl_3 + 3NaOH + 2H_2O \longrightarrow Fe(OH)_3 + 2H_2O + 3NaCl$$

COMPOUND	APPEARANCE
Iron Chloride	
Sodium Hydroxide	
Final Compound	

QUESTIONS:

1. Write out in words a chemical equation describing the double displacement reaction you just observed. _____

_____

2. Is the final substance the same as either of the two beginning substances? Why? _____

_____

_____

3. If any gas was given off during this reaction, what was it likely to have been? _____

_____

44

Date: _____ Names: _____

DECOMPOSITION REACTION

INTRODUCTION: If you pour baking soda into your hand and separate it into single "pieces," you still have baking soda. Heating baking soda, however, will cause it to separate into different compounds.

OBJECTIVE: In this activity, we will observe an example of a reaction in which a single substance gets broken down into several component parts. This is called a DECOMPOSITION REACTION.

PROCEDURE:
1. Pour 2 cm of baking soda into your clean, dry, PYREX test tube.
2. Using the test tube holders, hold the test tube over the flame. **Be careful to tilt the test tube at an angle and away from all lab group members.**
3. Observe the reaction and record your observations in the space provided below.
4. Conduct a carbon dioxide test by lighting a wooden splint in the flame, then placing the burning splint in the open end of the test tube. If the flame goes out, there is carbon dioxide present.

OBSERVATIONS: _____

_____

_____

_____

QUESTIONS:

1. Describe the color of the baking soda before and after the experiment.

    a. Before: _____ b. After: _____

2. Is there anything (besides baking soda) on the walls of the test tube? Describe. _____

_____

_____

3. If the equation for this reaction is $2NaHCO_3 \longrightarrow \uparrow CO_2 + Na_2CO_3 + H_2O$, where does the moisture come from? _____

_____

4. How many reactants are there in this reaction? _____ Name it/them. _____

5. How many products are there in this reaction? _____ Name it/them. _____

_____

6. Write out in words how the equation should be read. _____

_____

_____

7. What happened to the burning splint? Why? _____

_____

Date: _____   Names: _____

SYNTHESIS REACTION

INTRODUCTION: What happens when rust forms on steel? Where does the rust come from?

OBJECTIVE: In this activity, we will observe an example of a reaction in which a new substance is formed from several individual substances. This is called a SYNTHESIS REACTION.

PROCEDURE:

1. You are provided with 2 glass containers that are the same size. Label one A and one B.
2. In the bottom of the container labeled B stuff enough steel wool so that it will not fall out when the jar is turned upside down.
3. In the 2 large petri dishes (or pie pans) pour 1–2 cm of water. The amount is not important, just make sure both pans have the same amount.
4. Turn both glass containers upside down, and place one in each petri dish/pie pan of water.
5. Place both containers in an undisturbed spot for 5 days.
6. At the end of 5 days, observe both the water level in each container as well as the appearance of the steel wool, and record your observations in the space provided below.

OBSERVATIONS:

| | WATER LEVEL IN JAR | | WATER LEVEL IN DISH/PAN | | STEEL WOOL |
	Jar A	Jar B	Jar A	Jar B	
Set-up Day					
Day 5					

Date: _____ Names: _____

QUESTIONS:

1. Describe what happened to the water levels in the two dishes/pans.

    a. Dish/pan A: _____

_____

    b. Dish/pan B: _____

_____

2. Describe what happened to the water levels in the two jars.

    a. Jar A: _____

_____

    b. Jar B: _____

_____

3. What might account for this difference in water levels in the jars? _____

_____

_____

4. What happened to the steel wool? _____

_____

_____

5. What is the new product that was synthesized? _____

_____

6. Why was the empty jar set up along with the steel wool jar? _____

_____

_____

_____

Date: _____ Names: _____

SEPARATING A COMPOUND

INTRODUCTION: Of what two elements is water composed? If you splattered a tiny drop of water on wax paper and kept slicing it into smaller and smaller droplets, could you ever separate the drop into those two gases? What would it take to get the two gases apart?

OBJECTIVE: In this activity, we will break down the compound water by exposing it to an electric current. This process is called ELECTROLYSIS.

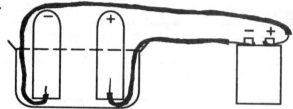

$$2(H_2O) \xrightarrow[\text{(electricity)}]{} 2H_2 + O_2$$

PROCEDURE:

1. Use the diagram below as a guide to help you set up the electrolysis apparatus you will be using.

2. Add 300 mL of water to your 400 mL beaker.

3. Label your test tubes (+) and (-). Then fill each tube with water and pour the water into a graduated cylinder to find its total volume. Record each total volume in the chart in the "Total Volume" space.

4. The test tubes should be filled with water, stoppered, and their tops submerged under the water in the beaker. When the stopper is removed under water, the water will remain in the test tube until forced out by the gases that are collected.

5. Connect the wires to the battery and run them through the water, placing one into each upside-down test tube. The (-) wire should go to the (+) tube and the (+) wire to the (-) tube.

6. For 5 minutes, observe any reaction in the water or test tubes. Record your observations in the observations section on the next page.

7. After the 5 minutes, add 1 heaping teaspoon of baking soda or 1 teaspoon of vinegar, stir gently, and observe again for 5 minutes. Record your observations.

8. Continue collecting the gases like this until about 10 minutes before class ends.

9. Remove test tubes by stoppering them under water (take wires out first) and removing them from the beaker.

10. Dry the outside of the tubes and mark the water line on each. Mark the tubes with a (+) or (-) to show which electrode from the battery went into each tube.

11. To measure the volume of water forced out of each test tube by the gas now present in them:
    a. Unstopper the test tubes.
    b. Pour the water from one tube into the graduated cylinder, and measure its volume as accurately as possible.
    c. Record this volume in the chart for "Final Volume."
    d. Subtract to find the amount of water displaced by gas.
    e. Repeat for the other test tube.

Date: _____ Names: _____

	TEST TUBE (+)	TEST TUBE (-)
TOTAL VOLUME		
FINAL VOLUME		
VOLUME OF GAS		
ELECTRODE ATTACHED: +/-		
TYPE OF GAS: H+ or O-		

OBSERVATIONS:

Water: _____

_____

Water with baking soda: _____

_____

QUESTIONS:

1. What do you think the purpose of the baking soda or vinegar was? _____

_____

_____

2. What is the relationship between the two volumes of gases? (Are they the same? Is one four

times the other?) _____

_____

_____

3. What do you think is the reason for this relationship? _____

_____

_____

4. How does this activity demonstrate that the formula for water is H_2O? _____

_____

_____

Date: _____   Names:_____

SEPARATING MIXTURES

INTRODUCTION: If you were at the beach and were thirsty and there was nothing but ocean water, how would you get rid of the salt from the water so you could drink it? What's one way to clean up oil spills? If you spilled a shaker of salt in the sand, but needed the salt to put on your food, how would you separate the sand and salt?

OBJECTIVE: In this activity, we will consider the different physical and chemical properties of substances that have been mixed together in order to figure out how to separate each pair of substances.

Complete the challenge before going on to the next page.

CHALLENGE: Think about and describe how to separate each of the following pairs of materials.

I. Oil and water suspension (oil and water shaken up):

_____

_____

_____

_____

II. Saltwater solution (salt dissolved in water): ** You must save both salt and water.

_____

_____

_____

_____

III. Salt and sand mixture: ** Both grain sizes are the same.

_____

_____

_____

_____

Date: _____ Names: _____

** CAUTION: No test tube should be heated unless it clearly has "Pyrex" written on it. **

PROCEDURE: <u>SEPARATING THE OIL AND WATER SUSPENSION</u>

1. Leave the suspension sitting very still until you have separated the other substances.

2. Use the pipette to siphon (suck) the oil from the top of the water and place it in a separate clean test tube.

** Label each of the separated tubes, and set them aside for instructor inspection.

<u>SEPARATING THE SALTWATER SOLUTION</u>

1. At your lab station, there are several pieces of equipment you will use to set up a distillation tube.

2. Place the hollow glass tube in the stopper.

3. Attach the hollow plastic tubing to the other end of the glass tube.

4. Place the stopper (with tubing attached) into the solution test tube.

5. The other end of the plastic tubing should be placed in a clean, empty test tube. **Do not** let the end of the tube go to the bottom of the test tube.

6. The solution test tube will be heated to evaporate the water and leave the salt behind.

7. Use test tube tongs to hold the solution tube about 4 inches above the top of your Bunsen burner, tilted at about 45 to 60° on its side, **away from people.**

8. Ask your instructor to light the Bunsen burner and heat solution until salt left behind is **reasonably** dry.

9. When heating is complete, place salt tube into test tube rack and shut off the gas to the Bunsen burner.

** Label both the salt and fresh water tubes and set them aside for instructor inspection.

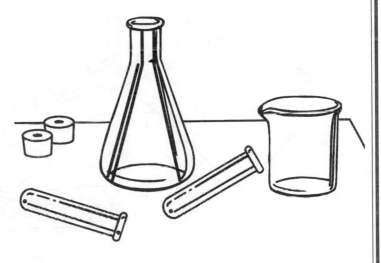

Date: _____ Names: _____

SEPARATING THE SALT AND SAND MIXTURE

1. First, the salt should be dissolved by adding about 5 mL of water to the mixture and stirring (by rolling tube between your palms).

2. Let the sand settle.

3. Pour the liquid into a separate clean test tube. (Steps 1 and 2 may need to be repeated if it looks like there is still lots of salt in your sand.)

4. **Do not heat sand test tube to dry the sand.** The sand is acceptable wet.

5. The saltwater tube should now be heated as in steps 1–8 in the previous section.

6. When the salt is **reasonably** dry, place the tube in the test tube rack and shut off the gas to the Bunsen burner.

** Label both the sand and salt tubes and set them aside for instructor inspection.

CLEAN-UP

1. After your instructor has inspected your test tubes, clean up your lab station and test tubes, put away the supplies that you used, and wipe the countertop.

    a. **No sand is to be poured into the sinks!**

    b. All test tubes should be washed with soap and test tube brushes.

Date: _____ Names: _____

QUESTIONS:

1. Why did the oil and water separate? _____

_____

2. What purpose did the plastic tubing serve when you distilled the salt water? _____

_____

_____

3. What different steps (of the "water cycle") does the distilled water go through to get to the other

test tube? _____

_____

4. Why doesn't the salt "go with" the evaporated water? _____

_____

5. Describe three "changes of state" from the three separations above. (Be specific.)

     a. _____

     b. _____

     c. _____

6. How would you separate salt from ocean water? _____

_____

_____

7. What is one (time-consuming) way to clean up oil spills? _____

_____

_____

8. How could you get the spilled salt out of the sand? _____

_____

Date: _____ Names: _____

MAKING SOAP

INTRODUCTION: Did you know that the very stuff we use to clean oils and dirt from our skin is made from animal fat (grease)?

OBJECTIVE: In this activity, we will use proper lab techniques to combine several substances over heat to make soap.

** THROUGHOUT THIS ENTIRE ACTIVITY, GOGGLES MUST BE WORN. RINSE SKIN IF SPLATTERS TOUCH IT. HEAT SLOWLY TO DECREASE RISK OF SPLATTERING.

PROCEDURE:

1. In a 250-mL beaker, pour 3 or 4 tablespoons of fat (lard or bacon grease).

2. Slowly add enough of the 10% sodium hydroxide (NaOH) solution to cover the fat with about 2 to 3 cm of NaOH.

3. Gently boil the mixture for 8–10 minutes.

4. Turn off the heat and allow the solution to cool for about 10 minutes.

5. ** At this point you may wish to add perfume/cologne for scent.

6. Add 2 tablespoons of salt and stir.

7. The soap will rise to the top of the solution.

8. Skim the soap off of the top with the spoon and place it on the wire mesh.

9. Rinse the soap under running water to remove excess NaOH, then form it into a ball and test it by trying to wash your hands with it.

QUESTIONS:

1. Describe the amount of soap that you made. _____

_____

2. Does this soap enable you to wash your hands? _____

3. What other industry might work well with the soap-making industry? _____

_____

4. What are some things that could be used instead of bacon grease to make soap? _____

_____

Date: _____ Names: _____

MAKING GOOP

INTRODUCTION: Have you ever wanted to play chemist and mix up something just to play with?

OBJECTIVE: In this activity, we will use household products to create a rubber-like substance.

PROCEDURE:

1. In the small pan, pour 100 mL of laundry starch.

2. Add 1 teaspoon of salt and stir it to dissolve as much as possible.

3. Squirt a small blob of Elmer's School Glue into this solution.

4. Use your fingers to thoroughly knead the glue so that all parts of its surface contact the salty starch.

5. ** Differences in measurement may cause you to need to add a tad more salt or glue to reach a Silly Putty consistency.

6. Remove the blob, that is the Goop.

7. Pour the extra laundry starch back into its supply container and rinse the pan.

THERE ARE NO QUESTIONS FOR THIS ACTIVITY. ENJOY YOUR GOOP AFTER CLEANUP!

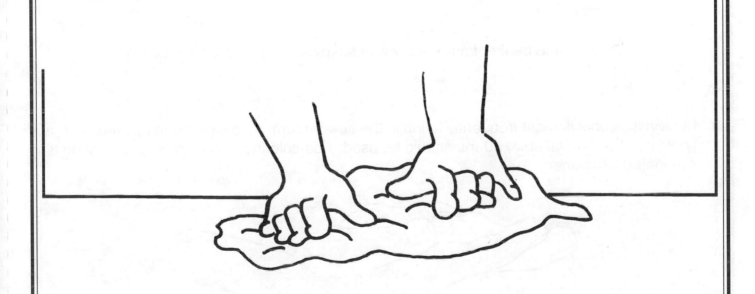

Date: _____ Names: _____

MAKING SLIME

INTRODUCTION: Did you ever wonder how they make that stringy, sticky slime that you can buy in some gumball machines?

OBJECTIVE: In this activity, we will use proper lab techniques to mix and heat several chemicals together in order to make slime.

PROCEDURE:

1. Measure out 15 g of polyvinyl alcohol and set it aside.

2. Heat 50 mL of water to boiling over the heat source.

3. At this point food coloring can be added for color. Use combinations of a total of 2 drops to make the desired colors.

4. Add the polyvinyl alcohol to the water, and remove the solution from the heat.

5. Stir continuously.

6. Add 1/2 teaspoon of sodium borate (Borax) while stirring.

7. ** The amount of Borax can be altered to determine how thick the solution becomes. The more Borax, the thicker the slime.

8. When the slime has cooled sufficiently, you can remove it from the beaker to handle it.

9. Clean the beaker immediately with soapy water and a beaker brush.

*** Polyvinyl alcohol is most frequently found in the powder form as described in this recipe. If a liquid solution is available, 50 mL should be used. Add coloring and then Borax. Heating is eliminated altogether.

Date: _____ Names: _____

CONSERVATION OF MATTER

INTRODUCTION: When you mix two chemicals that bubble and fizz, what happens to the stuff that "fizzes out"? Does it just go out into the air?

OBJECTIVE: Matter can change from one form to another, but cannot actually be created or destroyed. This is known as the LAW OF CONSERVATION OF MATTER. In this activity, we will investigate this concept using a chemical reaction.

PROCEDURE:
1. Soak an egg-sized piece of steel wool in vinegar for 4 minutes.
2. Remove the steel wool and wring out excess vinegar.
3. Place the steel wool in the flask (without rolling it into a ball).
4. Cover the mouth of the flask with a balloon.
5. Weigh the entire flask system and record the weight.
6. Sketch the flask system in the space provided below.
7. Set the flask system aside until the end of the period.
8. At the end of the period, reweigh the flask system.
9. Sketch the flask system again in the space provided below.
10. Record 3 observations in the space provided below.

OBSERVATIONS: _____

_____

_____

DATA: BEFORE   AFTER

WEIGHT:	WEIGHT:
SKETCH:	SKETCH:

QUESTIONS:
1. What happened to the balloon throughout the reaction? _____

_____

2. What happened to the weight of the system during the reaction? _____

_____

3. How does this activity illustrate the Law of Conservation of Matter? _____

_____

Date: _____   Names: _____

MASS, VOLUME, AND DENSITY

INTRODUCTION: Why do rubber ducks and boats float while submarines and rocks sink?

OBJECTIVE: In this activity, we will investigate how the mass of an object and the volume of the object are related. We will also calculate the density of several objects. The DENSITY of an object is defined as the number of grams in one cubic centimeter of a substance.

PROCEDURE:

1. At your lab station are 6 sealed containers; 3 are floaters and 3 are sinkers.
2. Determine the mass of each of the floaters/sinkers, and record it in the chart below.
3. Using the overflow containers filled with water, determine how much water is displaced by each floater/sinker. This can be done by pushing the floaters under water using forceps or by simply gently dropping the sinkers into the containers full of water. Measure the volume of the water that spills out into the pan.
4. Record volumes in the chart below for each floater/sinker.
5. Graph the data using (*) to represent floaters and (o) to represent sinkers.
6. Calculate the density of all 6 containers by using the formula: $D = \dfrac{M}{V}$

7. Record the density in the chart below. Also record your classmates' data on your graph.

DATA:

	FLOATERS			SINKERS		
	1	2	3	1	2	3
MASS						
VOLUME						
DENSITY						

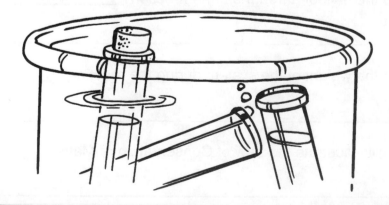

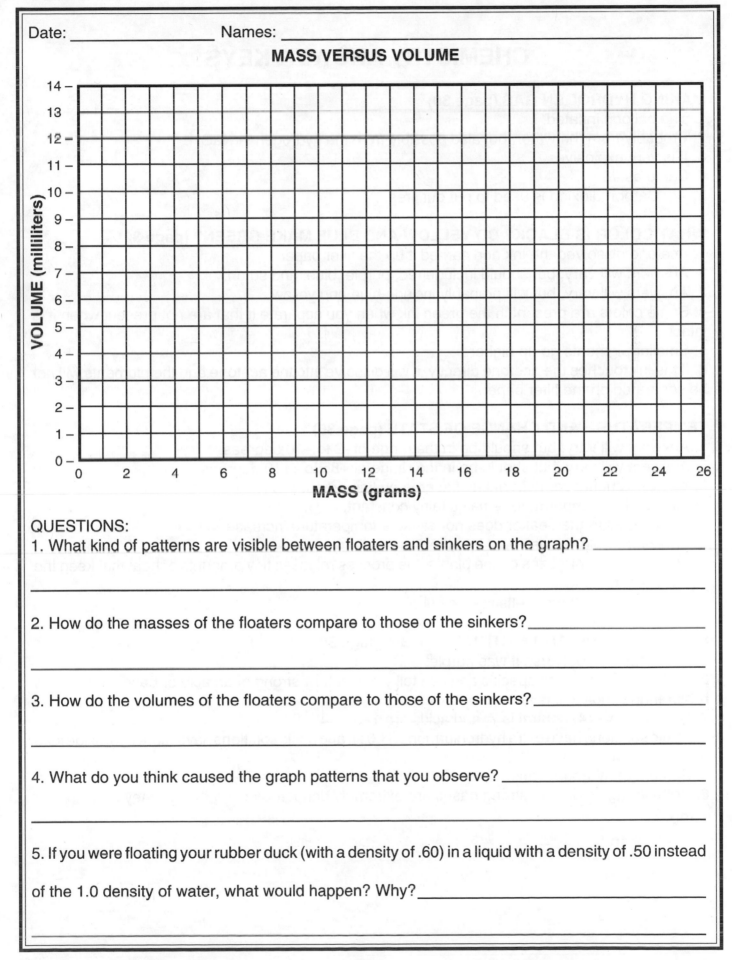

Date: _____   Names: _____

MASS VERSUS VOLUME

QUESTIONS:

1. What kind of patterns are visible between floaters and sinkers on the graph? _____

_____

2. How do the masses of the floaters compare to those of the sinkers?_____

_____

3. How do the volumes of the floaters compare to those of the sinkers?_____

_____

4. What do you think caused the graph patterns that you observe? _____

_____

5. If you were floating your rubber duck (with a density of .60) in a liquid with a density of .50 instead

of the 1.0 density of water, what would happen? Why?_____

_____

59

CHEMISTRY ANSWER KEYS

MAKING HYDROGEN GAS (page 30)
1. The balloon inflated.
2. Probably from the water, but also possibly from the hydrogen in NaOH.
3. It is very explosive.
4. Same as #3.
5. No. Carbon dioxide is used to put out fires.

WHAT COLOR IS BLACK? DO YELLOW AND BLUE MAKE GREEN? (page 32)
1. Acetone dissolved the ink and carried it up the filter paper.
2. Answers will vary, but should include red, purple, blue, and so on.
3. Answers will vary, but will probably include blue and yellow.
4. Some colors are present in the green ink when you separate it that are not present when it is intact.
5. Smaller pigments go up higher.
6. If the ink touches the acetone directly, it will dissolve into the acetone and the pigments will not be separated on the filter paper.

TEMPERATURE AND CHANGE OF STATE (page 35)
1. Answers will vary, but should be in the range of -2 to +10 degrees.
2. Answers will vary, but should be in the range of +85 to +110 degrees.
3. Answers should come from first flat area on line graph.
4a. and b. The temperature remains fairly constant.
5. Heat added to the beaker does not cause a temperature increase.
6. Freezing would release heat into the surroundings.
7. When the water freezes on the plants, the process releases tiny amounts of heat that keep the plants from freezing.
8. Heat from your hand melts the ice cube.

INDICATORS, pH, AND NEUTRALIZATION (page 39)
1. It was neither, because it was purple.
2. Litmus paper is more specific and can tell you just how strong of an acid or base a solution is rather than simply if it is an acid or base.
3. Bases are 8–14, neutral is 7, and acids are 1–6.
4. Acidic solutions have extra hydronium ions (H_3O+), and basic solutions have more hydroxide ions (OH-).
5. Percent of hydrogen ions.
6. Both strong acids and strong bases are extremely dangerous even though they may appear clear.

TEMPERATURE EFFECTS ON SOLUBILITY (page 42)
1. Answers will be based on the hypothesis and data.
2. Higher temperature liquids generally dissolve more solid.
3. Solvent: water, Solute: salt.
4a., b., and c. Each of these will be extrapolated from the graph of data.
5a., b., c., and d. Each of these will be extrapolated from the graph of data.
6. The highest temperature recorded will dissolve the most sugar.

SINGLE DISPLACEMENT REACTION (page 43)
1. Silver nitrate plus copper yields copper nitrate plus silver.
2. Single displacement
3. The copper replaces the silver on the nitrate complex and frees the silver ion.

DOUBLE DISPLACEMENT REACTION (page 44)
1. Iron chloride plus sodium hydroxide yields iron hydroxide plus sodium chloride.
2. No. The first ion on each compound has traded places.
3. Hydrogen.

DECOMPOSITION REACTION (page 45)
1a. White; b. Whitish-yellow
2. There is moisture on the walls of the test tube (and maybe some black carbon residue).
3. The moisture is the water that results from the bicarbonate breakdown in the baking soda.
4. One. Baking soda (sodium bicarbonate)
5. Three. Carbon dioxide, sodium carbonate, and water
6. Sodium bicarbonate yields carbon dioxide plus sodium carbonate plus water.
7. The splint went out because it was exposed to carbon dioxide.

SYNTHESIS REACTION (page 47)
1a. A small amount of evaporation may have occurred.
 b. More water will be missing from pan B than from pan A.
2a. The water level will remain equal to that in the pan.
 b. The water level in the jar will be higher than that in the pan.
3. Air pressure decreased in the jar as oxygen was used to form rust allowing more water to be pushed into the jar.
4. Rust formed on the steel wool.
5. Iron oxide
6. The effects of rusting on oxygen use and water levels could be compared to the control, where the only thing affecting water levels would be evaporation and air pressure.

SEPARATING A COMPOUND (page 49)
1. The baking soda allowed electricity to flow through the water more easily.
2. The hydrogen bubble should be about twice the volume of the oxygen bubble.
3. There are twice as many hydrogen atoms as oxygen atoms in each water molecule.
4. Twice the volume of hydrogen appears in the collection tube demonstrating that H_2O means there are two hydrogen atoms for each oxygen atom.

SEPARATING MIXTURES (page 52–53)
1. Oil is less dense than water.
2. It carried the steam across to the collection tube and allowed it to condense into water.
3. Evaporation, condensation, precipitation.
4. Salt does not evaporate at the same temperature as water.
5. Answers may vary: a. salt dissolves; b. water evaporates; c. water vapor condenses.
6. Distill the ocean water and collect the precipitant.
7. Suction the oil from the surface of the water.
8. Dissolve the salt with water, pour the salt water off, and evaporate the water from the salt.

MAKING SOAP (page 54)
1. Answers will vary.
2. Answers will vary.
3. Meat packaging plants might sell fat that is trimmed from meat to soap makers.
4. Lard or other animal fats could be used.

CONSERVATION OF MATTER (page 57)
1. The balloon slowly gets pushed into the flask.
2. The weight should not change (much).
3. There are obvious changes going on in the system such as the change in color of the steel wool and the balloon getting pushed into the flask as the reaction occurs, but the mass of the system does not change.

MASS, VOLUME, AND DENSITY (page 59)
1. Floaters are located in the upper left corner of the graph while sinkers are located in the lower right corner.
2. Masses of floaters are less than masses of sinkers.
3. Volumes of floaters are greater than volumes of sinkers.
4. If the volume of an object is greater than its mass, it floats. If the mass is greater than the volume, it sinks.
5. A rubber duck with a density of .60 would sink in a liquid with a density of .50 because the density of the duck is greater than the density of the liquid (its mass is greater than its volume).

PHYSICS INDEX AND MATERIALS LIST

Date: _____   Names: _____

RADIOACTIVE DECAY: HALF-LIVES

INTRODUCTION: Suppose you fill a shoe box with 20 heads-up pennies. If you shake the box, how many pennies would you expect to be heads up? If you take out all the tails-up pennies and then shake the ten (or so) heads-up pennies, how many do you expect to land heads up this time? How about next time?

OBJECTIVE: Radioactive materials tend to lose their radioactivity over time by emitting radioactive particles. This process is called RADIOACTIVE DECAY. The time it takes a radioactive substance to decay ranges from a few days to millions of years. The rate of radioactive decay is measured in HALF-LIVES. A half-life is the length of time it takes a radioactive sample to lose half its radioactivity. In this activity, we will simulate radioactive decay and examine the rate at which a "radioactive sample" loses its radioactivity.

PROCEDURE:

1. At your lab station, you will find a cup of 50 cardboard chips that are yellow on one side and gray on the other side. Yellow side up represents radioactive material. Gray side up represents nonradioactive or "decayed" material.

2. The 50 chips represent 50 radioactive atoms of an element.

3. Place all 50 chips in cup with yellow sides up (radioactive).

4. To simulate the time equal to one half-life passing, cover the cup with your hand and shake the cup vigorously.

5. Dump the contents of the cup onto the table top.

6. Remove all the "decayed" gray atoms and put them aside.

7. Count the remaining "radioactive" yellow atoms, and record this number in the chart as "Half-Life #1, Trial 1."

8. Place the radioactive atoms back into the cup, yellow side up, and repeat for half-life #2. Continue through half-life #7 or until 0 or 1 atom remains.

9. Repeat the entire process for two more trials, beginning each time with 50 yellow-side-up chips in the cup.

10. When all three trials have been completed, total the number of radioactive atoms remaining at each half-life and then divide by 3 to find the average.

11. Graph the average number of radioactive atoms versus the half-life number on the graph sheet provided.

Date: _____ Names: _____

DATA:

HALF-LIFE #	TRIAL 1	TRIAL 2	TRIAL 3	TOTAL	AVERAGE
1					
2					
3					
4					
5					
6					
7					

RADIOACTIVE ATOMS VERSUS HALF-LIFE

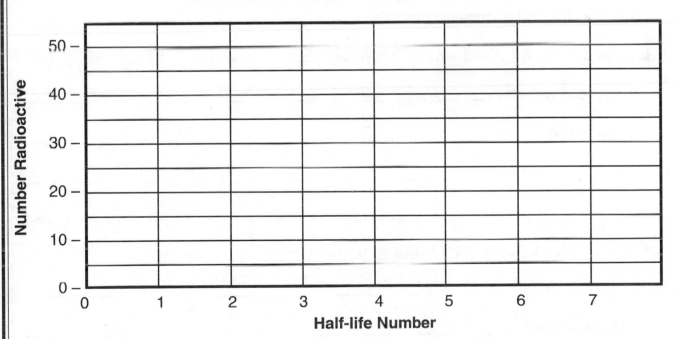

Date: _____ Names: _____

QUESTIONS:

1. What does half-life mean? _____

_____

2. When starting with 50 radioactive atoms, how many remain radioactive after four half-lives?

_____

3. What if you had started with 100 radioactive atoms? How many would remain radioactive after

four half-lives?_____

4. How many half-lives are needed to reduce the number of radioactive atoms to:

     a. one-half the original number? _____

     b. one-fourth the original number? _____

     c. one-eighth the original number?_____

     d. one-sixteenth the original number?_____

5. If you start out with a 1,200-gram radioactive sample, how much is still radioactive:

     a. after one half-life? _____

     b. after two half-lives? _____

     c. after three half-lives? _____

     d. after four half-lives? _____

6. How many of the 20 pennies are heads up after:

     a. one half-life (shaking)?_____

     b. two half-lives? _____

     c. three half-lives?_____

Date: _____ Names: _____

INSULATION

INTRODUCTION: If your house had no heat, what would you rather use to cover up and keep warm with? Nothing, not even clothes? Aluminum foil? Newspaper? Plastic wrap? A thick wool sweater?

OBJECTIVE: Different materials allow heat transfer to occur more easily than others. Materials that allow heat to transfer from one area to another very easily are called CONDUCTORS. Materials that do not allow heat transfer are called INSULATORS. In this activity, we will investigate the insulating abilities of several different materials.

PROCEDURE:

1. Get the following set-ups ready to insulate the 4 cups/cans at your lab station as:
   a. Control (no cover, no wrapping).
   b. Covered all around with aluminum foil.
   c. Surrounded by wadded up newspaper (1–3 inches thick).
   d. Packed in styrofoam packing chips.

2. Add 200 mL of hot water to each can.

3. Complete insulating each can as described in step 1.

4. Take a starting temperature of each insulated can (allowing about 30 seconds for the thermometer to stabilize) and record each in the chart below.

5. Continue taking temperature readings every minute for 15 minutes and recording the temperatures in the chart below.

6. Graph each set of data on the graph provided. Color coordinate the 4 data lines using colored pencils. (Control = black, Foil = blue, Paper = red, Styrofoam = green)

TIME IN MINUTES

INSULATING MATERIAL	Start	1	2	3	4	5	6	7	8	9	10	11	12	13	14	15
Control																
Foil																
Newspaper																
Styrofoam																

Date: _____ Names: _____

TEMPERATURE VERSUS TIME

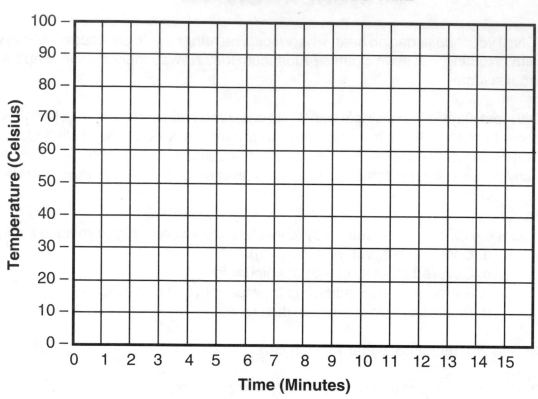

Temperature (Celsius)

100 –
90 –
80 –
70 –
60 –
50 –
40 –
30 –
20 –
10 –
0 –

0 1 2 3 4 5 6 7 8 9 10 11 12 13 14 15

Time (Minutes)

QUESTIONS:

1. Which insulation allowed the greatest cooling? _____

2. What characteristic do you think caused this substance to insulate worst? _____

_____

3. Which insulation allowed the smallest amount of cooling? _____

4. What characteristic do you think helped this substance insulate best? _____

_____

5. Why was one can left uncovered and unwrapped? _____

_____

6. Which item was the control in the list of items for keeping warm in your unheated house?

_____

Date: _____ Names: _____

SPECIFIC HEAT AND KINETIC ENERGY

INTRODUCTION: What happens when you rub your hands together? What causes the warming that you feel? Is there a different amount of warming when you rub your hands longer? Harder?

OBJECTIVE: POTENTIAL ENERGY is stored energy. KINETIC ENERGY is energy of motion. In this activity, we will convert the potential energy of sand into kinetic energy. This will be done by shaking the sand vigorously. The increase in its temperature is evidence of kinetic energy. The specific heat of a substance is the amount of heat energy needed to raise the temperature of that substance one degree. In this activity, we will observe how the mass of a substance affects its specific heat.

PROCEDURE:

1. Fill one styrofoam cup 1/2 full of sand (estimate).

2. Insert the thermometer into the sand and take a starting temperature reading.

3. Place a second cup upside down over the first and tape it in place with masking tape (temporarily).

4. Shake this system vigorously for 1 minute.

5. At the end of 1 minute, disassemble the cups and measure the ending temperature. Record your data in the chart below.

6. Repeat steps 2–5 for: a full cup of sand—1 minute.
                             1/2 cup of sand—2 minutes.
                             a full cup of sand—2 minutes.

7. Calculate the temperature change by subtracting the starting temperature from the ending temperature.

AMOUNT OF SAND	TIME	STARTING TEMP.	ENDING TEMP.	TEMP. CHANGE
1/2 Cup	1 minute			
Full Cup	1 minute			
1/2 Cup	2 minutes			
Full Cup	2 minutes			

Date: _____ Names: _____

QUESTIONS:

1. What kind of energy is represented by:

   a. sand sitting still?_____

   b. moving sand?_____

2. What evidence is there that energy changes from potential to kinetic during the activity? _____

_____

3. Describe other examples of:

   a. potential energy. _____   _____

   b. kinetic energy. _____   _____

4. What did you do that changed the potential energy into kinetic energy?_____

_____

5. Of the two 1-minute tests, which cup increased in temperature the most? Why? _____

_____

6. Of the two 2-minute tests, which cup increased in temperature the most? Why? _____

_____

7. Of all four tests, which cup increased in temperature the most? Why? _____

_____

8. Which of the following objects would require the LEAST amount of heat to increase its temperature? (Circle one.)

   a. 1 gram of lead   b. 10 grams of lead   c. 100 grams of lead

Why? _____

9. How does the mass of a substance affect its specific heat? _____

_____

_____

REFLECTION

Date: _____   Names:_____

INTRODUCTION: How do you know where to hit the backboard to get a basketball to bank into the basket? How do you figure out where to bank a shot off the side of a pool table in order to get the ball to go into the pocket? Basketballs and billiard balls behave in certain ways when they strike a solid object, and so does light.

OBJECTIVE: Since light travels in straight lines, when it strikes objects through which it cannot pass it bounces off the object or REFLECTS. In this activity, we will use a marble to represent moving light, and we will examine how the angle at which light hits an object (INCIDENT ANGLE) affects the angle at which the light bounces off of the object (ANGLE OF REFLECTION).

PROCEDURE:

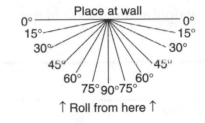

1. At your lab station you will find a colored sheet with angles drawn on it. The angles are measured from 0° to 90° and back to 0°.
2. Place the 0° angles against the back wall of the countertop or the wall of the classroom (as shown in the diagram at the right).
3. For each angle listed in the chart below, roll the marble toward the center of the grid along the mark that represents that angle and repeat 2 times.
4. Observe the angle at which the marble bounces off the wall, and record this angle as the angle of reflection in the chart below. **If a marble is mistakenly rolled at the wrong angle, simply repeat that trial until the marble rolls down the appropriate line and strikes the center of the grid.**
5. Find the average angle of reflection by adding the 3 trials for each incident angle to get a total and then dividing the total by 3.
6. Record the average data in the chart below.

INCIDENT ANGLE	ANGLE OF REFLECTION TRIAL 1	TRIAL 2	TRIAL 3	TOTAL	AVERAGE ANGLE OF REFLECTION
15°					
30°					
45°					
60°					
75°					
90°					

71

Date: _____ Names: _____

QUESTIONS:

1. In this activity, what represented:

    a. the incident angle? _____

    b. the angle of reflection? _____

2. How do the incident angle sizes and angle of reflection sizes in your data compare?

_____

_____

3. How do the directions of the incident angles and angles of reflection in your data compare?

_____

_____

4. In general, a definition of reflection based on this data might read:

"Reflection occurs when an object/light bounces off of another object at the _____

angle, but in the _____ direction."

5. A basketball that needs to bounce off at a 40° angle on one side of the goal should be thrown

at what angle on the opposite side of the goal? _____

Date: _____ Names: _____

CONCAVE AND CONVEX LENSES

INTRODUCTION: The bottom of a broken soft drink bottle forms a circular piece of glass that is thicker in the middle than at the edges. If you looked through this, what effect would this "lens" have on the appearance of objects? If you could only see things close up and needed to have things far away made larger to see them, what kind of lens would you need in your glasses? What if you could only see far away and needed things up close made smaller to see them? What kind of lens would you need in your glasses?

OBJECTIVE: CONVEX and CONCAVE lenses refract (bend) light so that images appear different than they actually are. In this activity, we will use drops of water to construct both a convex and a concave lens, and then we will observe the effect of each lens on printed words.

PROCEDURE: <u>CONCAVE LENS</u>
1. Turn your plastic cup upside down.
2. Spread petroleum jelly on one side of the rubber washer.
3. Place the greased washer on the bottom of the plastic cup (avoid any letters or indentations on the bottom of the cup).
4. To make a concave lens, place 2–3 drops of water inside the center of the washer. There should be just enough water to stretch entirely inside the washer **as thinly as possible. It might be easiest to fill the inside of the washer and then remove as much water as possible to leave just a thin layer of water.**
5. Move the cup over the letters on this lab sheet and observe the effect of the "lens" as you look through the water droplet.
6. Describe your results in the chart on the next page.

<u>CONVEX LENS</u>
7. Repeat steps 1–6 above, **except:**
    a. In step 4, to make a convex lens, place 2–3 **more** drops (for a total of 4–6 drops) into the center of the washer. There should be enough water to pile up over the edges of the washer without spilling over.

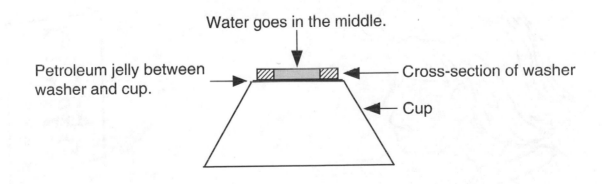

Water goes in the middle.

Petroleum jelly between washer and cup.

Cross-section of washer

Cup

Date: _____   Names: _____

LENS	OBSERVATIONS (APPEARANCE OF PRINT)
Concave	
Convex	

QUESTIONS:

1. What kind of effect does a concave lens have on the appearance of objects? _____

_____

2. What kind of effect does a convex lens have on the appearance of objects? _____

_____

3. Sketch a side view of a:

     a. concave lens.   b. convex lens.

4. Which lens above would be used for:

     a. farsightedness (can see far away but not up close)? _____

     b. nearsightedness (can see up close but not far away)? _____

Date: _____ Names:_____

PINHOLE VIEWER, or "HOW THE EYE WORKS"

INTRODUCTION: If we could look into your eye to see what you see, we would see objects upside down inside your eye.

OBJECTIVE: Light travels in straight lines. This allows scientists to predict how it will behave as it passes through and is bent by objects (REFRACTION) and as it bounces off of objects (REFLECTION). In this activity, we will construct a set-up to observe refraction and another device to observe the effects of reflection of light after it travels in straight lines through a pinhole (as it does when it enters the pupil of the eye).

PROCEDURE: <u>REFRACTION</u>

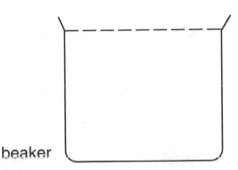

beaker

1. Fill a beaker with water and place a plastic ruler in it.
2. Observe the beaker and ruler from the side.
3. Sketch what you observe in the space at right.

<u>REFLECTION</u>

4. Place a piece of tracing paper over the opening of the metal can provided, and secure it in place with a rubber band.
5. Place the candle in the pan or on the aluminum provided away from the back of the counter and away from this lab sheet and other paper.
6. Have your instructor light your candle. (If it goes out later, you may light it from your neighbor's candle.)
7. The metal can has a tiny hole in its closed end. Turn this end toward the candle flame about 4 inches from the flame so that the side of the flame faces the pinhole. **See Diagram A below.**
8. Move the can around so that the light from the candle becomes visible on the tracing paper through the can.
9. Observe the direction that the top of the flame is pointing. It may be helpful to gently fan the flame so that it moves at its top.
10. In Diagram B, sketch the flame as it is seen on the tracing paper.
11. In Diagram C, draw the side view of how the light must pass through the can to cause the flame tip to point as it is. Use straight lines to represent the movement of light.

DIAGRAM A

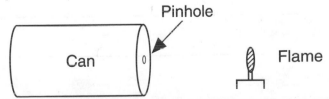

Pinhole

Can   0   Flame

Date: _____ Names: _____

DIAGRAM B

DIAGRAM C

QUESTIONS:

1. What direction is the candle flame pointing? _____

2. Why is the candle pointing the way it is? _____

_____

_____

3. Is the image on the tracing paper "screen" the same size as the actual flame? _____

4. What might account for the difference in the size of the image? _____

_____

_____

5. Compare the pinhole viewer to the human eye. Which part of the viewer is similar to:

    a. the pupil? _____

    b. the retina? _____

Date: _____ Names: _____

ELECTRICAL CIRCUITS

INTRODUCTION: How do the batteries, bulb, and wires in a flashlight connect to get the bulb to burn? Why do Christmas tree lights often go out when one lightbulb burns out? Why can you turn off one light in your house but leave other lights on?

OBJECTIVE: An electrical circuit is the pathway through which electricity flows. In order for devices like light bulbs to burn, the circuit must be closed—there must be a continuous flow of electricity along conductors with no interruption. When a circuit is opened, the flow of electricity is interrupted (the circuit is broken), and the lightbulb turns off. Devices like light switches, knife switches, and circuit breakers or fuses are used to open the circuits. In this activity, we will construct three types of circuits. The first circuit is a simple circuit in which only the bare necessities will be used so that points of contact may be observed. In the final two circuits, series and parallel, more equipment will be used and usefulness will be investigated.

PROCEDURE: SIMPLE CIRCUIT

1. At your lab station, you will find many wires, bulbs, and ceramic sockets as well as switches. For this activity, you may use only the following: **one bulb, two wires, and one battery.**
2. Experiment with connecting those four items together in order to get the lightbulb to light up.
3. When the light burns, **show** your instructor and **sketch** this simple circuit in the space below. (Show exactly where wires touch bulb and battery.)

- -

SERIES CIRCUIT

4. Using any of the materials provided, construct the series circuit diagrammed below.
5. Include a knife switch, "XXXX," as is shown in the diagram.

Date: _____ Names: _____

QUESTIONS:

1a. What happens when the knife switch is up? _____

 b. With the knife switch up, is the circuit open or closed? _____

2a. What happens when the knife switch is down? _____

 b. With the knife switch down, is the circuit open or closed? _____

3. What happens when the knife switch is down and one light bulb is unscrewed from its ceramic base?

_____

4. What might you have encountered that acts the same way when one light goes out?

_____

- -

PARALLEL CIRCUIT

6. Using any of the materials provided, construct the parallel circuit below.

7. Insert a knife switch, "XXXX," as in the diagram.

QUESTIONS:

5a. What happens when the knife is up? _____

 b. When the knife switch is up, is the circuit open or closed? _____

6a. What happens when the knife is down? _____

 b. When the knife switch is down, is the circuit open or closed? _____

7. What happens when the knife is down and one lightbulb is unscrewed from its ceramic base?

_____

8. What is the advantage of this parallel circuit over the series circuit? _____

_____

Date: _____ Names: _____

** CHALLENGE

I. Connect your series circuit with your neighbors' circuit to create a series circuit with 1 switch and 4 bulbs. Sketch below.

SUPER SERIES CIRCUIT:

- -

II. Connect your parallel circuit with your neighbors' parallel circuit to create a parallel circuit with 1 switch and 4 bulbs. Sketch below.

SUPER PARALLEL CIRCUIT:

Date: _____   Names: _____

WHAT CONDUCTS ELECTRICITY?

INTRODUCTION: What would happen if you used aluminum foil to wire a circuit for flashlight batteries and a bulb? Would the bulb light? What if you used nylon string or your braces instead?

OBJECTIVE: In this lab, you will investigate which types of substances act as CONDUCTORS (allow the flow of electricity) and which substances act as INSULATORS (resist the flow of electricity).

PROCEDURE:

1. Set up a circuit that includes a battery, a lightbulb and ceramic base, and 3 pieces of wire as shown in the diagram below.

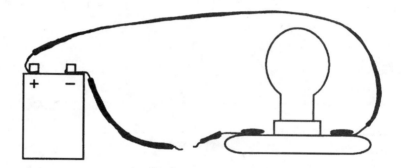

2. Test the circuit to see if it is complete by attaching the two loose wires (where there is no insulation). If the circuit is complete (light comes on), proceed below.

3. In the chart on the next page is a list of items that will be tested for conductivity. For each item, make a hypothesis as to whether the result will be positive or negative, and record the hypothesis in the chart. A positive result means that the bulb burns and the substance is a conductor. A negative result means that the bulb does not burn and the substance is an insulator.

4. To test each item, touch one of the loose wires to one end of the object and the other loose wire to the other end of the object.

5. Record your results in the chart.

80

Date: _____ Names: _____

OBSERVATIONS:

OBJECT	HYPOTHESIS	RESULT (+/-)	CONDUCTOR OR INSULATOR
a. copper wire			
b. penny			
c. nickel			
d. wood splint			
e. rubber stopper			
f. glass rod			
g. tap water			
h. salt water			
i. baking soda water (base)			
j. colored water			
k. chalk			
l. charcoal			
m. a piece of jewelry			
n. aluminum foil			
o. acid			
p. pencil lead			
q. your finger			
r. braces (if you dare)			
s. your choice #1			
t. your choice #2			

QUESTION:

1. What characteristic did most of the "conductors" share? _____

_____

Date: _____ Names: _____

MAGNETS

INTRODUCTION: What makes magnets stick to your refrigerator? Why does rubbing a nail with a magnet cause the nail to become a magnet, too?

OBJECTIVE: Magnets are created when the atoms of a substance are altered to align all the individual atomic charges in similar directions—with all positive charges in one direction and all negative charges in the opposite direction. The opposing charges create the "opposites attract" situation in which the NORTH side of a magnet is attracted to the SOUTH side, while like sides repel each other. This alignment can be created by exposure to electricity, contact with other magnets, or by impact. In this activity, we will investigate the attractive and repellant forces of magnets as well as the magnetic field surrounding the magnets.

PROCEDURE: <u>TESTING MAGNETIC POLES</u>
1. To determine which side of the magnet is North, move the arrow end of your compass around the magnet. The side of the magnet that the red arrow points toward is North. The opposite side is South.
2. Mark your magnet sides N and S.

<u>MAGNETIC FIELD LINES</u>
3. In the next 3 steps, you will conduct the test on a separate sheet of paper and then sketch your observations in the space provided on this sheet (smaller than your actual results).
4. Single magnet:

paper on top

   a. Place a single magnet on its side on the counter.
   b. Lay your blank sheet of paper across the top of the magnet. **(See left)**
   c. Sprinkle (lightly) the surface of the white paper with iron filings 2–3 inches away from the magnet in all directions.
   d. Sketch the magnetic field lines below:

Date: _____ Names: _____

5. Two attracting magnets: a. Place two magnets, opposite sides facing, on the counter. **(See left)**

b. Repeat steps 4b–d and sketch your results below:

N| |S N| |S

paper on top

6. Two repelling magnets: a. Place two magnets, like sides facing, on the counter. **(See left)**

b. Repeat steps 4a–d and sketch your results below:

S| |N N| |S

paper on top

Date: _____ Names: _____

MAGNET STRENGTH

7. Test the strength of your magnet by hanging paper clips end-to-end from the bottom of the magnet. Record the total number of paper clips in the chart below.
8. Repeat this test with both magnets "stuck together" to see if the number of magnets affects magnetic strength.

NUMBER OF MAGNETS	NUMBER OF PAPER CLIPS (STRENGTH)
1	
2	

QUESTIONS:

1. What happens in materials to cause them to become magnetized? _____

_____

_____

2. What three things commonly cause magnetism?

    a. _____

    b. _____

    c. _____

3. What is the general shape of magnetic field lines? _____

_____

4. Does the number of magnets have a significant effect on magnetic strength? What is your evidence?

_____

_____

5. What happens to a nail that is rubbed by a magnet that causes it to become a magnet?

_____

_____

Date: _____ Names: _____

MAKING AN ELECTROMAGNET

INTRODUCTION: How do cranes use magnets to move scrap iron in junkyards? How do they get those huge pieces of iron off of tho magnet once they get it on the magnet?

OBJECTIVE: Electricity can be used to temporarily align the "magnetic domains" within a piece of iron in order to create an electromagnet. In this activity, we will use an iron nail, copper wire, and a battery to construct an electromagnet that will then be tested to determine how the number of wraps of wire around the nail affect the strength of the electromagnet.

PROCEDURE:

1. Wrap the copper wire around the nail the designated number of times—allowing at least about 4 inches at each end of the wire for connecting to the battery.

2. Connect the ends of the wire to opposite poles of the battery. This will complete the circuit through thc wiro and create the electromagnetic field that will in turn magnetize the iron nail.

3. To test the strength of the electromagnet, touch paper clips to the nail.

4. "Stick" as many paper clips to the nail as possible for each number of turns of wire around the nail and record the maximum number in the chart on the next page.

5. Remove all paper clips from the nail, add 5 more turns of wire, and test with paper clips for the strength ot the electromagnet.

6. Continue through all the designated numbers of wire turns.

7. **Graph the number of wire turns versus the number of paper clips on the graph provided.**

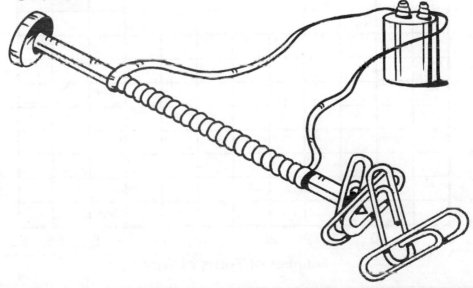

Date: _____   Names: _____

DATA:

# TURNS OF WIRE	# OF PAPER CLIPS
5	
10	
15	
20	
25	
30	
35	
40	
45	
50	
55	
60	

NUMBER OF TURNS VERSUS STRENGTH

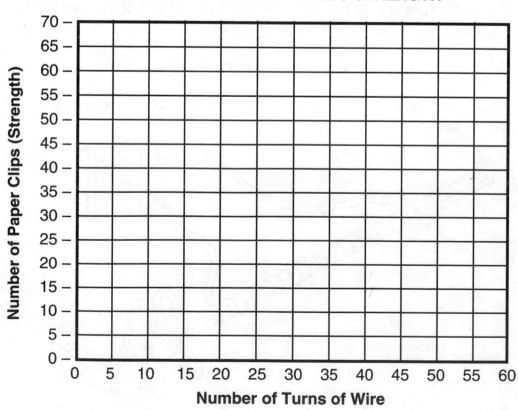

© Mark Twain Media, Inc., Publishers

Date: _____   Names: _____

QUESTIONS:

1. According to your data, how does the number of turns of wire affect the strength of the electro-magnet?

_____

_____

_____

2. What happens to the electromagnet when the wires are disconnected from the battery?

_____

_____

_____

3. What does the electricity do to the nail to cause it to become a temporary magnet?

_____

_____

_____

4. What is an advantage of an electromagnet over an ordinary permanent magnet?

_____

_____

_____

5. What kind of problem would you have if you used a permanent magnet strong enough to pick up huge pieces of scrap iron?

_____

_____

_____

Date: _____   Names: _____

TIN CAN MOTOR

OBJECTIVE: In this activity, we will construct a motor from a used soup can, two magnets, a battery, two paper clips, a thread, some tape, and a few wires.

PROCEDURE:

1. Straighten 2 large paper clips and place them on opposite sides of the open end of the soup can.

2. Attach **attracting** magnets to the upper end of the paper clips.

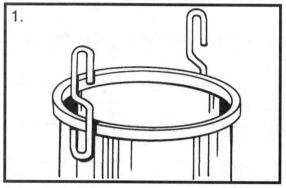

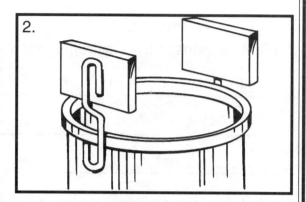

3. Measure 2 pieces of 24-cm-long wire and strip 4 cm of insulation from all 4 ends.

4. Wind one end of each wire around a pencil to form a closed loop.

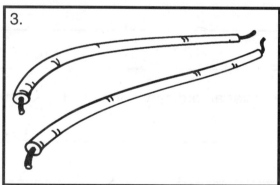

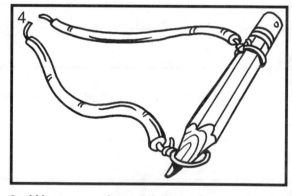

5. Place these loops above the rim of the can between and at the same height as the magnets.

6. Wrap another 24-cm piece of wire around a D battery, then remove it.

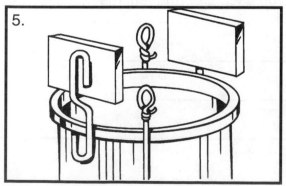

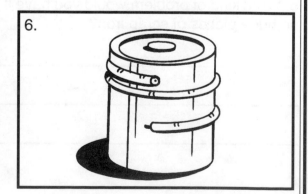

Date: _____   Names: _____

7. Tightly loop each end of the wire. Then peel the insulation off of the arms of the coil.

8. Tie a thread to the loop on one side and wind it around twice. Tape its end and trim the excess.

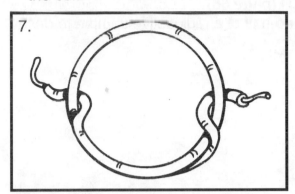

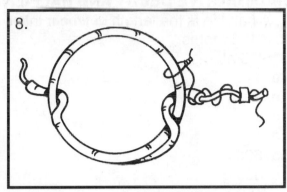

9. Shape the coil so that it is balanced. Place it in the two loops between the magnets.

10. Connect the two long ends to opposite electrodes of the battery. Blowing the coil should start the motor. You might need to reverse the coil to start it spinning.

11. Discuss how the thread makes the coil spin.

PHYSICS ANSWER KEYS

RADIOACTIVE DECAY AND HALF-LIVES (page 66)
1. A half-life is the length of time it takes one-half of a radioactive sample to decay.
2. 3.125 atoms
3. 6.25 atoms
4a. 1
 b. 2
 c. 3
 d. 4
5a. 600 g
 b. 300 g
 c. 150 g
 d. 75 g
6a. 10
 b. 5
 c. 2.5

INSULATION (page 68)
1. Answers may vary.
2. Will probably include answers such as: "The substance was very thin," "The substance conducts heat," or "The substance wouldn't stay around the cup well."
3. Answers may vary.
4. Will probably include answers such as: "The substance had lots of air spaces," "The substance stayed up next to the cup well," or "The substance was very thick."
5. The uncovered/unwrapped cup served as a control with which comparisons could be made.
6. Nothing at all, not even clothes.

SPECIFIC HEAT AND KINETIC ENERGY (page 70)
1a. Potential energy
 b. Kinetic energy
2. The temperature of the sand increases.
3a. Answers may vary but will include examples of objects at rest.
 b. Answers may vary but will include examples of objects in motion.
4. The movement of the sand created friction between the grains of sand.
5. Answers may vary, but the expected result is that the 1/2-full cup will increase in temperature most. This is due to: a. smaller mass is easier to increase in temperature; and b. more room to move inside the cup leads to greater friction.
6. Same as #5.
7. Answers may vary, but the expected result is that the 1/2-full cup in the 2-minute test should increase the most. This is due to: a. smaller mass is easier to increase in temperature; b. more room to move inside the cup leads to greater friction; and c. more time is available to allow for more friction.
8a. 1 gram of lead. This is due to the smaller mass. It takes less heat energy to increase the temperature of a smaller mass.
9. The smaller the mass of substance, the lower its specific heat.

REFLECTION (page 72)

1a. The incident angle is the angle at which the marble is rolled toward the wall.
  b. The angle of reflection is the angle at which the marble bounces off of the wall.
2. Incident angles and angles of reflection are similar (very close in size).
3. The directions of the incident angle and angle of reflection are opposite. If the marble is rolled from one direction, it bounces off in the other.
4. same, opposite
5. 40 degrees

CONCAVE AND CONVEX LENSES (page 74)

1. Concave lenses cause the object to appear smaller.
2. Convex lenses cause the object to appear larger.
3a. Concave: b. Convex:

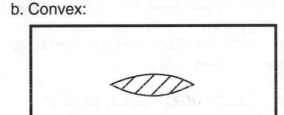

4a. concave
  b. convex

PINHOLE VIEWER, or "HOW THE EYE WORKS" (page 76)

1. Upside down
2. Light travels from the top of the flame through the hole in a straight line and ends up low on the tracing paper. Light travels from the bottom of the flame through the hole and ends up near the top of the tracing paper. This happens because light travels in straight lines.
3. No.
4. The distance of the pinhole viewer from the flame changes the angles between the straight lines crossing at the hole in the can, causing different sizes of images on the tracing paper. The closer the viewer to the flame, the larger the image.
5a. The hole
  b. The tracing paper

ELECTRICAL CIRCUITS (page 78)

1a. The lights go off.
  b. The circuit is open.
2a. The lights turn on.
  b. The circuit is closed.
3. Both lights will be off.
4. Christmas tree lights will sometimes behave like this. When one burns out, they all go out.
5a. The lights go off.
  b. The circuit is open.
6a. The lights turn on.
  b. The circuit is closed.
7. The remaining bulb will continue to burn.
8. In a parallel circuit, some items can be turned off without turning off everything in the circuit.

WHAT CONDUCTS ELECTRICITY? (page 81)
1. Most conductors are made of metal.

MAGNETS (page 84)
1. Objects become magnetized when the individual atoms within the substance are aligned so that all positive charges point in one direction and all negative charges point in the opposite direction.
2a. Contact with other magnets
  b. Electricity
  c. Impact
3. Answers may vary, but expected answers are that magnetic field lines point outward where the magnetic field is strongest and curve between those areas.
4. Answers may vary, but generally speaking the number of magnets does not increase the strength of the magnetic field. This is observed as the same number of paper clips is picked up by one or two magnets.
5. The atoms in the nail all become arranged so that positive ends point one way and negative ends point the opposite way.

MAKING AN ELECTROMAGNET (page 87)
1. The more wire wrapped around the core (nail), the stronger the electromagnet.
2. When wires are disconnected, the electromagnet loses its power.
3. The electricity aligns the atoms with the core so that all positive charges point in one direction and all negative charges point in the opposite direction.
4. Electromagnets can be turned on and off to pick up things and release them, and they can also be made very strong.
5. If a permanent magnet was strong enough to pick up the iron, it would be almost impossible to get the iron off of the magnet.